A
Therapeutic
Atlas

Published in 2022 by The School of Life
First published in the USA in 2023
930 High Road, London, N12 9RT

Copyright © The School of Life 2022

Designed and typeset by Marcia Mihotich
Printed in Latvia by Livonia Print

A proportion of this book has appeared online at
www.theschooloflife.com/thebookoflife

The School of Life is a resource for helping
us understand ourselves, for improving our
relationships, our careers and our social lives
– as well as for helping us find calm and get
more out of our leisure hours. We do this
through creating films, workshops, books,
apps and gifts.

www.theschooloflife.com

ISBN 978-1-912891-93-1

10 9 8 7 6 5 4 3 2 1

MIX
Paper from
responsible sources
FSC
www.fsc.org   FSC® C002795

A
Therapeutic
Atlas

The School of Life

43/55 ●

37 ●
    15 ● ● 14
    60 ● ●45/57
         ● 7
  41 ● 59 ● 1
         ● 33
         49 ●
    53 ● ● 6
50 ●
  54 ● ● 18

● 30

10 ●   ● 36
42 ●   ● 5
   47/52 ● 16/24

● 48
● 25
17/34 ● ● 19
35 ● ● 26

● 8

● 51

● 3

● 11

● 58

● 56

22

46

44

31

13

23

2

2

27

39

29

28

38

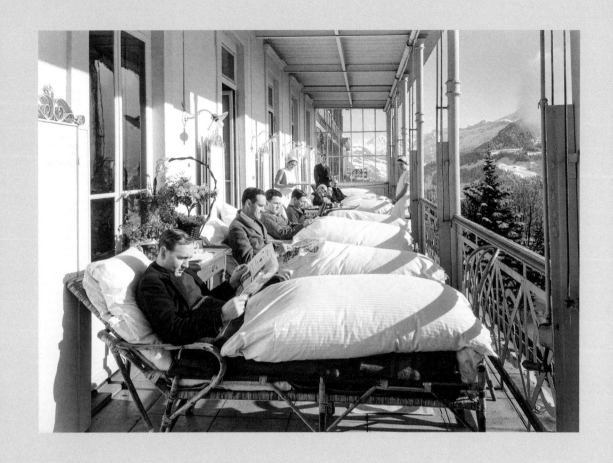

A healing gallery at l'Hôtel du Mont-
Blanc, Leysin, Vaud, Switzerland, c. 1950.

A sanatorium – and landscape –
to combat tuberculosis.

Introduction

Ideally, we would never have to leave the house, or even our bed. It would all be to hand – everything one desired, needed and hoped for would be within immediate reach, as it might have been when one was very small and at peace in a comforting cradle.

But as we mature, our needs invariably develop in more complicated ways and so the ability of a single environment to meet them must falter. We start to dream of 'elsewhere'; we want to go places; we crave a change of scene.

We've been doing this for a long time. The ancient Greeks were among the first to know about therapeutic places – the word stems from their term θεραπευτικός, *therapeftikós*, meaning curative, helpful, healing – and they constantly took to the road in the hope of finding relief: they went to the Sanctuary of Asclepius in Epidaurus to beg for help for piles and cancer, wind and earache; they went to the Oracle at Delphi in search of wisdom and advice on marriage and career; they went to the Temple of Poseidon at Cape Sounion to derive courage and counsel on seafaring; and in addition had a hundred or so major shrines around the Greek world to choose from to address problems ranging from impotence and infertility to depression and insomnia.

Our species has continued to look out for therapeutic places to travel to. In the 1840s, the German doctor Hermann Brehmer discovered that patients with tuberculosis might be helped by spending many months at high altitude, largely lying horizontally on an outdoor terrace facing the sun. And so, for over a century, until the discovery of streptomycin, the Alps were dotted with imposing sanatoria with large glazed balconies overlooking pastures ringing with the sound of cow-bells and dedicated to the management and eradication of *Myco-bacterium tuberculosis*.

Other places have been recommended to treat ailments of a more diffuse psychological nature. Eighteenth-century doctors prescribed that the bereaved should visit Karlsbad in Bohemia (present-day Karlovy Vary) to drink at least ten glasses of water a day from the springs; the mineral-rich waters at Baden-Baden were reputed to have the power to console the childless and those abandoned in love.

We don't need to be convinced believers in religion or adherents of the woollier ends of medical treatment to recognise the overall point: that there are places that can help, parts of the world that can assist us with our troubles in a way that our own homes cannot. This book is a compendium of therapeutic places that may offer us a holiday or respite from certain difficulties of our psyches; places that can help us to reframe our difficulties, shed new light on our mental blocks, lift our moods and restore us to a measure of calm and purpose.

We are all patients in various states of distress, some of us hobbling, the rest of us bravely keeping up appearances. Every worthwhile location is – in a sense – a sanatorium to which we should repair for moments of rest and inspiration; a place where we might stop for a while, in our imaginations or in reality, in order to rebuild our strength and identify a few new reasons to live.

Places
of the Mind

Tower of Silence, Wind Towers and
Ice Chamber, Yazd, Iran.

We constantly need evidence of
'otherness' to open up new horizons
in our minds.

Elsewhere

Before we even get to any of their specific qualities, many places end up feeling therapeutic for a reason as simple as it is essential: because they are first and foremost symbolic of 'elsewhere'. They are valuable because they speak of a departure from everything that is normal and habitual for us – at a point when our spirits and powers of imagination have become depleted and we are on the verge of losing faith because of all that we know.

We go abroad and thrill at distinctive new buildings, lights, customs, clothes, accents, flavours, names and road signs. We do so not only for these elements themselves, but because they hint to us in a broader way about the idea of alternatives. They are reminders that we cannot have exhausted all possible options, given that so much that is unexpected and unheralded still exists – and therefore the world remains a far broader, more unpredictable and more option-rich place than we had assumed in our despair.

Central to many states of sadness is a feeling of predictability. We sigh because things are bad right now, but also because we believe we know the rest of the story, for all time: the marriage will not improve, there will be no way out of our professional difficulties, we can't picture how our enemies would stop gossiping, society seems utterly set in its ways, daft ideas will permanently be granted prestige, our melancholy will never lift. A sense of 'sameness' isn't an accidental feature of sad moods; sadness is underpinned by the sapping belief that what is now will always have to be.

It may not matter too much what sparks the reminder of the idea of 'elsewhere'. It could be the sound of Danish on the streets of Aalborg, the smell of thyme and cinnamon in the markets of Fez, a poster in downtown Hôi An written in the Vietnamese alphabet (*Chũ Quôc ngũ'*), or the light at dawn in the Atacama Desert. Or it might be time spent reflecting on the mud-and-brick Towers of Silence in central Iran, some of the most haunting and peculiar buildings in the history of the world's least-known major faith, Zoroastrianism. We might look at the structures – originally used to lay out the bodies of the dead for birds of prey to strip the flesh from the bones – and be stirred by an evocation of all the odd details of Zoroastrianism that still await our discovery: the worship of the god-like deity Ahura (Lord) Mazda (wisdom); the belief in the conflict between *asha* (order and reason) and *druj* (chaos and lies); the faith in a saviour figure called Frashokereti who will bring about a time of renewal when the souls of the dead will be weighed and the righteous will enter a paradisiacal land called Kshatra Vairya; and the veneration of a holy book called the *Avesta*. These are the tenets of the world's first monotheistic faith, which came to prominence 2000 years before Christianity.

We are not really fed up with life, only with the tiny slice of it that we know and that has (understandably) disappointed us in too many ways. We need contact with an 'elsewhere' to dislodge us from sterility and reawaken us to wonder. We need to surprise and dehabituate ourselves back to health.

Urbano Monte (Monti), Map of the
World (detail), 1587.

It can help us a lot to look at
a map that's all 'wrong'.

Terra Incognita

When we're travelling around the world, it helps hugely to use maps that have accurately and comprehensively worked out the real features of the landscape. When we're more broadly going around our minds, it can be just as helpful to encounter maps that have holes in them: maps where not everything is fixed, maps that allow for surprising and unusual speculations, maps with time for the odd monster or unicorn, maps with unknown regions left on them, maps that appreciate how badly we need to have some 'terra incognita' left to play in.

One of the more inspiring maps in this regard was completed in 1587 by the Italian geographer Urbano Monte. Even though he spent fifteen years on the map and consulted with hundreds of travellers and sailors in order to draw it, it is beautifully and touchingly 'wrong' about a great many things. Australia is an extended lump off Antarctica, Japan is almost joined up with Alaska, the estuary of the Amazon is seven times its real size, there's deep confusion around the scale of the Indonesian islands. There are fantastical creatures dotted everywhere: mermaids off the Gulf of California, flamingo-like birds in Tierra del Fuego, giant bearded men wrestling with one another in the Andes, rhino-like beasts marauding through Namibia – and lots of unicorns here and there. And then, where even Monte's imagination runs out, he simply puts in clumps of (European) trees, flowers and scatterings of apologetic 'terrae incognitae'.

The map would be a mess to use to sail around the globe, but it's a delight to contemplate, in part because we are so asphyxiated day to day by how much appears to be known and is alleged to be immovable. This is the way we're meant to educate children, this is how relationships are supposed to be, this is the sort of job it is correct to have … Yet, in truth, a vast amount remains utterly unforeseen, not around maps, but in existence as a whole. We struggle to know what our collective purpose should be, we can't securely grasp what we're trying to be educated in and for, the ultimate aim of increased wealth is opaque, no one understands how relationships work and why they simply don't most of the time, loneliness and fear remain endemic. Technology can't deliver much of what we would want of it; the human animal appears as demented, restless and unkind as it ever was.

How useful, therefore, to let a very old and wonky map make a point in visual form that we have trouble holding on to as an idea in our minds: that no one really knows. They know bits, here and there. But in key areas, where it can really count, there is a remarkable original ignorance still at play, an insight as frightening as it is emancipating. We don't continually have to subscribe to authority. We don't have to believe in experts in areas where there aren't any. We can trust more in our own minds and give greater credence to certain of our authentic wishes. Monte's unicorns and misshapen continents are, despite their quirks, directing us with great accuracy to an actual destination: a place where we understand that we are a lot more free than we thought we were.

Aerial view of the Ideal City of
Chaux, Arc-et-Senans, France.
Engraving after a drawing, from
Claude-Nicolas Ledoux, *L'architec-
ture considerée sous le rapport de
l'art*, Vol. I, Paris, 1847.

This was his ideal place. We should
dream up examples of our own.

Utopia

Some of the most important places we could visit are those that exist as yet only in dreams: speculative landscapes and cities summoned up by utopian thinkers who have tried to imagine how we should ideally live, how our houses should ideally look, what we should ideally value and how we should ideally love. The places may not be real, but they are something more important still: they excite us to want to alter present reality in the name of a more tolerable and fulfilling future.

The utopian French 18th-century architect Claude-Nicolas Ledoux dreamt of cities that would be better than those where he had lived and worked. He wanted to create places that would be harmonious, sociable, egalitarian and elegant, and over a number of years designed an ideal settlement, which he pictured taking shape in the wooded region of Chaux, near Besançon in eastern France. He mapped out spacious residential avenues, inspiring public squares, a House of Union where people could meet in the evenings, and a Temple of Memory where they would commemorate the dead and celebrate the changes of the seasons. The Chaux city never came into being, but its example provokes us still to ask ourselves – amidst our own urban mess – what cities should be like and what we could improve if we were not so inert and in thrall to traditional arrangements.

An accusation of 'utopian thinking' can sound like an insult; we are meant to pride ourselves on being grounded, realistic and sober. Insofar as we dare to imagine the future, we do so with one peculiar tic: we cautiously ask ourselves what the future will be like on the basis of current trends. We almost never ask the one big, philosophically minded question: what *should* the future be like? We proceed as humble futurologists, viewing what is to come as something to be guessed at, rather than as bolder and more directive utopian philosophers,

laying down a blueprint for what we want to happen.

Or else we believe that because we cannot master all the practical challenges in the way of a better future, we have no right to dream of it. But that is to give too privileged a place to obstacles and too small a role to the imagination, which must always come prior to, and can be independent of, the subsequent work of realisation.

We should dare to open up a utopian strand to our reflection – and to our mental travels. We should clarify our dissatisfactions with what exists by asking ourselves in detail: what sort of better world can we journey to? What would the streets be like there? How would marriage be arranged, how would children be brought up, what would mass entertainment promote?

We almost certainly have all the ingredients of our own utopias present in our minds already, but a shyness holds us back from focusing on them to the extent that they might evolve into a plan. We mustn't only sigh about how things are. We should travel in our minds to how they should, and could one day, be.

Remondini Family, *Description of the Land of Cockaigne, Where Whoever Works the Least Earns the Most*, 1606.

We should fantasise about what our land of happiness might look like.

The Land of Cockaigne

Throughout the medieval and early modern periods, one of the most popular travel destinations was the land of Cockaigne. It was sometimes believed to lie on an island below Spain; at other times, it was situated in the Caribbean. More usually its location was left pleasantly vague – though there was general agreement that the weather there was always mild and the flora and fauna perfectly suited to human needs (often, as here in the top right-hand corner, guinea fowl would fly right out of the sky and onto people's plates for dinner).

According to one depiction produced by the Remondini printing firm in Italy in 1606, in Cockaigne money rained down from the sky, the lakes were filled with wine, crops harvested themselves, oxen ploughed fields unattended, the mountains were made of sugar, trees grew candied fruit, castles were fashioned out of gingerbread, streets were paved with pastry, ships were laden with pasta – and anyone who tried to do any work ran the risk of being arrested for disturbing the peace.

It might sound merely eccentric, but that would be to miss the significance and psycho-logical importance of that much-neglected and unprestigious activity: day-dreaming. Our era thinks of dreams only as things we should conjure up in order to bring them to fruition through immense hard work. But that is to misunderstand what dreams are for. Our far wiser ancestors knew that many dreams have no chance of ever coming into being – but that we need to spend time with them neverthe-less, in order not to go wild with frustration at our constricted conditions and the inevita-ble delays between desire and gratification. Dreams keep us going; they immerse us in more bearable scenarios so that we can return with greater strength to those obstacles we can't, for now, avoid.

It is part of the genius of the way our brains are structured that we don't necessarily need direct physical contact with things to derive their benefits. The thought alone can – sometimes – be enough. You can imagine a balmy afternoon in a field in Cockaigne and, for a moment, feel the sun's reviving rays while hearing the distant sounds of a gurgling brook of Chianti or Barolo and anticipating eating a mattress-sized snack of panettone.

Our medieval ancestors knew very clearly where their dreams took them: towards food, warmth and rest. Whatever its fanciful excesses, the land of Cockaigne provides us with an only-too-real map of everything that was missing from their desperate lives. Different things will be missing from ours. Each of us has a land of Cockaigne in our mind already, even if we haven't necessarily yet explored it or recognised it as such. When despair weighs on us, we should ask ourselves naïve but critical questions: what's Cockaigne for us? What do we want to gorge ourselves on? What would our lakes be filled with? What do we want to grow on trees? We should beware of surrendering our dreams too brutally or quickly in the name of realism or so-called maturity; daydreaming about what we really long for is a sensible way to get through the barren stretches.

Frederic Edwin Church, *Morning
in the Tropics*, c. 1858.

Our memories provide us with a huge
range of travel destinations that
we can access at no cost and with
total ease.

Travelling in Memory

We can suffer from an unfortunate and stubborn conviction that the only way to access the goodness of certain places is – on every new occasion – to take our bodies there; to buy a plane ticket, pack a suitcase and transport our material frame around the globe to reach what we need to see. It can't be enough to have visited one beach at one point; we have to keep returning to a beach every time we want to savour what a beach can be. Its benefits are assumed to last as long, and only as long, as the trip itself. The moment our toes have left the sand, the experience must be over.

But this is to fail to appreciate how ingeniously built our minds are and, in particular, what awesome powers of memory and evocation we possess – even if we normally only use these very haphazardly and meekly. Our minds forget more or less nothing, down to minute details. Almost everything that we have ever experienced has been dutifully recorded and shelved somewhere in the vaults of our memories. It's all still there: the smell of snow on the first day in the mountains of the Engadine, the taste of the vine leaves in the taverna near Rhodes, the sensation of a pair of childhood sandals, the tilework in the hotel in Aswan, the scent of roses in the garden in Ravenna. It's only habit and inattention that prevent us from regularly accessing these memories and summoning them to consciousness to derive some of their original advantages. Nevertheless, at times they will press themselves on us anyway. As we try to fall asleep, a memory of a trip a decade before may suddenly – unbidden – enter our minds. A smell may trigger a cascade of impressions we had given up ever knowing again; an entire period of childhood can be summoned up by contact with a certain kind of biscuit, sunlight or texture of carpet.

The 19th-century American painter Frederic Edwin Church made two journeys to South America in his lifetime; to travel like this across continents was enormously expensive and dangerous. Most people never even left home. The trips were relatively short, but what counted was how assiduous Church later was in tending to the memories of what he had seen and felt. Throughout his life, he would return in his head to places he could not go back to in body. He completed dozens of pictures of the trip up to two decades after he had come home. Thanks to his imagination, he could be both in his farmhouse in the Hudson Valley and, simultaneously, in Brazil, experiencing – as if it were happening in front of him – the light rising on the Amazon in the early morning.

Not being in a place should never hold us back from immersing ourselves in what it once made us feel. It is unfairly heavy-handed of us to think that we need always to keep travelling with our entire cumbersome selves; we should open up a far larger role for trips via memory. We should sometimes let our imaginations do what they have been designed for.

John Singer Sargent, *Two Boys on the
Beach with Boats*, c. 1878.

The problem with actually going
to places is that we have to take
ourselves with us.

Travelling without Me

The American artist John Singer Sargent went to Capri for the first time in 1878, when he was 22 years old. He was at once enchanted. He loved the olive groves, the turquoise seas, the little restaurants and the whitewashed houses. He had a short, loving relationship with a working-class woman called Rosina and made a number of paintings of her – and of the nature and buildings of the island.

One of the first, almost automatic, responses to seeing Sargent's landscapes is to be overwhelmed by a simple certainty: *I want to go there (ideally very soon)*. How could we not, when the waters look so extraordinarily inviting; when we can imagine lolling in the turquoise shallows, then drying out on a towel on the beach by the rocks? Perhaps we will have brought a little picnic and will have some goat's cheese and a *sfogliatelle* while looking out at the glittering horizon. Later in the afternoon, we might take a boat out to a nearby cove. In the evening, we might fall asleep to a full moon and the sound of cicadas. At last, here, we would be happy.

No one can contest the perfection of the images. But what we are in danger of forgetting is a huge inconvenience associated with going anywhere on the basis of an enchanting visual impression: that, if we were actually to go, each of us would have to take our self along. That 'self' is really a way of describing everything that makes being who we are so difficult day to day: all our depressive tendencies, compulsions, confusions, anxieties and sorrows. Certainly we would be faced with resplendent beauty, but we would also – more tragically – be looking at it through the smeared lens of our own maddening character.

This is one drawback that we are spared so long as we look at images of beautiful places in a book or on a screen. The act of looking is brief enough and the troublesome aspects of our personalities restrained enough that, for a few moments, we can immerse ourselves in the perfection of our surroundings without distortion, in a way that would – paradoxically – be impossible if we actually had to be there.

Were we by some mixed fortune to end up on a Capri beach, we would probably be troubled by our digestion, irritated by our lack of sleep, pained by a cut on our knee and upset by a sarcastic exchange with our partner. No such impediments need to worry us while we flip through a carefully selected set of images for a few minutes before dinner: we can be more 'there' than when we have to be there.

Without quite meaning to, images trick us. We might be more able to savour a place when we aren't faced with the additional hurdle of having to stand for hours in the enervating heat in the company of our own absurd, immovable personality. We don't, in reality, simply want to go to beautiful places; we want – more confusingly – to do so without 'me' in tow. We want a break from the appalling burden of being ourselves. We should fully appreciate that pictures have their advantages.

Jim Dow, *The Town Diner interior,
US 20, Watertown, Massachusetts,*
1979.

We aren't just being shown a nice
place; we're being taught how to
open our eyes.

Places of Appreciation

We're often under the impression that there is something inevitable and automatic about the way we decide that certain places are beautiful and worth visiting. It seems – for example – simply normal to want to go and look at Amsterdam or New York, the fields of Provence or the coast of Normandy, the lonely motels of America or the cafés of Paris.

Yet this is to overlook the extent to which our sense of what is beautiful has been actively moulded for us over time by artists whose work has guided our eyes – and made it possible for us to perceive a charm or interest in places that we might have walked straight past had we not been inducted with grace and expertise into their virtues. It may seem as if artists simply show us reality, but there is no such thing as reality per se, only an infinite number of possible realities from which a great artist will make a careful selection in order to tease out a vision that possesses particular interest and profundity. They will choose only certain times of day. They will discard all but a few kinds of light, they will crop their images to throw our attention on a very specific spot – and as a result of their labours, a beauty that might otherwise have remained latent, and fatefully mixed in with all that is humdrum and dispiriting, forgettable and offensive, is extracted like a precious metal from its ore, released, flourishes and then becomes impossible for us not to see.

We may think that we have chosen our itineraries, but it is, in truth, Van Gogh who has helped to give us the wish to go and see Provence, Vermeer and de Hooch who have incited in us a wish to visit the Netherlands, Monet who has taught us to appreciate the Normandy coast, Edward Hopper and Robert Frank who made us want to travel the lonely roads of rural America, and Caillebotte and Pissarro who gave us instruction on how to love the streets of Paris.

What makes Jim Dow's image of a diner in Watertown, Massachusetts particularly apt is that it is both a place that we would very likely have dismissed as utterly banal, and yet also one which, under Dow's quiet tutorship, we can come to recognise as distinctly dignified and seductive. The charm was always there. Dow (like other good artists) didn't make it up – he isn't an advertiser – but he had to identify it and throw it into relief. Our eyes had to be led to notice the solemnity of those coffee and tea dispensers and the general modest refinement of this chrome-plated machine for catering.

The pity is that there remain so many parts of the world that are beautiful and inter-esting, but that lack the artists who could help us appreciate them. We may have seen a lot already, but there is still so much more to notice.

Friedrich Overbeck, *Italia and Germania*, 1828.

What country might we need to fall in love with to complete ourselves?

Places of Completion

It's a hugely fanciful but importantly instructive picture. The young woman on the right is Germania; she's got fair skin and light-coloured hair and behind her is a Gothic cathedral and a castle typical of her country. Next to her on the left is Italia, a dark-haired maiden with a Tuscan-style village church visible beyond her shoulder. Judging by the way they are holding hands and sitting intensely next to one another, the two women have also fallen deeply in love – though, because it was 1828, the distinguished painter Friedrich Overbeck couldn't put it exactly like that to his audience. They were just very good friends.

The picture brings to the fore, in a way that later, more sophisticated works might not, a basic truth about our relationship to other lands: we are sometimes drawn to them in the way that we might be to a person. Crucially, the way we choose the country to venerate is similar to the way we may identify a partner. We frequently look to fall in love with people who will, in some way, be able to 'complete' us: that is, make up for a gap in our personalities and render us whole through their complementary skills and traits. If we are shy, it may be their confidence and bravery that entice us; if we are somewhat chaotic, their order and precision may prove the locus of our desire.

The same search for completion may be present in our attraction to countries. A Brazilian may find themselves filling a void in their personality by spending time in Norway; the streets of Tromsø may bring them a peace and diffidence that those in Campos dos Goytacazes do not. A Swiss national from Appenzell might connect with missing parts of themselves in Peru's Páucar del Sara Sara. And, for centuries, as Friedrich Overbeck made clear, many Germans have felt that Italy contained elusive or under-represented parts of their own natures, with which they wanted to become familiar.

In asking someone what country they feel ready to love, we are learning – first and foremost – about what elements of personality they value, but don't securely possess, and therefore need to bolster. Some of what we are seeking through our journeys is to mature and correct our imbalances: like Italia and Germania, we are looking to become whole by uniting with a foreign land.

The severed head of St Catherine
of Siena, Basilica San Domenico,
Siena, Italy, 1383.

One used to travel from afar to see
her for help with impotence; what
lands might fortify us now?

Places of Pilgrimage

For hundreds of years, across Europe, there was really only one reason to go travelling: in order to visit a shrine to a long-dead saint who might, if we prayed deeply enough and had the right sum of money, help us to get over a range of ailments of mind or body. Europe was covered with sites rendered sacred and therapeutic through association with a saint, whose bodily remains – normally entombed or framed within a costly display case – formed the centrepiece of a pilgrimage. The Catholic Church had a catalogue of shrines available, depending on the nature of the affliction. Women having trouble breastfeeding would be advised to travel to Saint-Sauveur Basilica in Rocamadour in southwestern France (you could buy supplies of the Virgin Mary's breast milk). Sufferers from headaches were directed to St Agathius' bones in the Basilica of the Vierzehnheiligen in Bad Staffelstein in Bavaria. And those who had sexual problems were commonly told to seek assistance from the remains of St Catherine of Siena, which were widely spread around Italy: one of her ribs being found in Florence, three fingers and a foot in Venice, a shoulder blade in Rome and – most spectacularly – her whole, unusually well-preserved head in an ornate reliquary at the back of the Basilica San Domenico in Siena.

Today we seldom believe in the power of saintly places to cure us, but we continue to trust, in a vague but plausible way, that there might be places that could work a curative effect on our troubles. We don't want to travel only in order to get away; we want to return as different people. We might, in an entirely secular spirit, think of updating (even if only for ourselves) the Catholic Church's catalogue of therapeutic destinations. There might be a small village at the foot of a glacier that could help us to rediscover perspective; there are cities that can revive specific ambitions; there could be a lemon grove that would silence the negative inner voices.

The ideal travel agent of the future wouldn't simply offer bargains or convenient itineraries. They would take the full measure of the sicknesses of our psyches and attempt to match these to a landscape with a power to loosen our hold on despair or sadness. There could be secular equivalents to the abbey church in Conques in southern France – recommended to soldiers lacking courage – or the Jesuit church in Antwerp containing the remains of St Apollonia, the patron saint of teeth. The pilgrims of old may have been eccentric in the details of their hopes, but they were astute enough in sensing that there could be locations that might redeem and assist them. We should take care to wander the earth with an atlas of therapeutic places to guide us.

Travelling

Tom Hegen, *Frankfurt Airport*, 2020.

Airports aren't just places to get
us to other places; they deserve to
be honoured as destinations in their
own right.

The Airport

They have become – quite unfairly – associated with aggravation and ugliness, but more imaginatively considered, airports are among the most impressive structures ever put up by our wretched species. If we were tasked with showing a visiting Martian the best of human capacities, we could do worse than to take them to the airport for a look around.

We are, for the most part, messy, indolent, querulous and irrational animals, but in the operations of an airport, we put our better sides forward: our powers of foresight, temperance, reason and ingenuity. At home we might shout, despair, curse and degrade, but within the airport precinct, only our more inspiring strengths are encouraged to emerge. We carefully track and help bring down a 200-tonne airliner approaching the airfield at 150 knots in a rainstorm; we inspect the fan blades inside an engine that was – only a few hours ago – firing across northern Greenland at temperatures of 1,700°C; we fill two under-wing tanks with 230,000 litres of Jet A-1 to carry 400 people and their luggage to Los Angeles at Mach 0.85.

Within ordinary conversations, we suffer from no end of misunderstandings; we devote hours to unpicking the gap between what someone said and what they might actually have meant. But there are no such ambiguities on the runways and aprons. An otherwise taciturn and heavily accented Bulgarian pilot will at once understand a German controller who tells them: 'Taxi to runway three four; hold short of Delta,' and there will be no one in the hundreds of aircraft on the move who won't immediately know what is at stake in the command: 'Heading two three zero, runway two seven left.'

Everywhere in the airport, awesome powers are involved: 72,000 pounds of thrust are being shot onto the runway as a Hanoi-bound 777's nose points skywards, and fourteen wheels, each one weighing some 109 kilograms, prepare to leave the ground. Yet the rage is contained, logical, utterly within parameters. No one loses their temper; there is a serenity at the heart of the inferno. A pilot can bring a 73-metre-long hull the size and weight of many houses to within a millimetre of its designated stop zone. It is like the hand of a giant caressing the brow of a child.

Humans, so unimpressive singly, are united in a collective effort to produce a spectacle of rare dignity. Airports are the cathedrals or the Roman aqueducts of our time.

There is further hope because of how easy it feels here to escape our present reality. There are endless planes begging to carry us elsewhere. The screens are blinking with flights for Montevideo and Tbilisi, Jakarta and Lusaka; the names alone have a poetry to them. We don't necessarily need to go anywhere; it's simply immensely reassuring to feel that we could.

The future may have disappointed us in many ways. It is ugly, disputatious and remarkably slow; we're still waiting for jetpacks and eternal life. But out at the airport, there is an alternative futuristic world waiting for us, showing us what it might be like if human beings could overcome their obtuseness and live up to the promises of technology. Though we may be in a hurry to reach our destinations, we don't necessarily need to go any further than we have; this might have been the best bit of the journey already.

Edward Burtynsky, *Cape Coral,
Florida*, 2012.

The further up we climb, the more
lovable our species becomes.

The Earth from the Air

The show through the familiar ovaloid window is seldom ever quite the same. On some flights, it features immense horizons illuminated a burning pink by a sun setting somewhere at the edge of a continent. On others, we're in pitch blackness interrupted only by a thousand stars and an occasional sibling aircraft streaking ruby-red beneath us. On certain journeys, we are granted vistas over the endless icy emptiness of northern Canada or Mongolia; on others, all we can see is a misty ocean traversed, every now and then, by an oil tanker or cargo ship the size of a full stop.

Whatever the particularities, these views belong to a unitary category of place that is as universally ignored as it is important, consoling and redemptive: *the earth from above*. How seldom we pay it the slightest attention; our forebears would have been astonished and even frightened by our nonchalance. They wouldn't have been able to stop staring. Leonardo da Vinci and Poussin would have relentlessly sketched the formations of cirrus and cirrostratus clouds; Galileo and Newton might never have recovered their footing. And yet, how quick we are to pull down the blind irritably so that we can more clearly follow the story on our screen of two people pretending to fall in love, while outside, a pair of Rolls-Royce Trent 1000s carry us over the forbidding 8,586-metre peak of Mount Kanchenjunga.

Humans are notoriously hard to bear at proximity: the closer we are to them, the more they madden and disappoint. Misanthropy is an almost inevitable response to a walk through an average shopping mall. But from up here, our species appears endearing, even sweet. Look at how we build our nests; look at how our motorways wind carefully around our warehouses and how our houses line up in pristine grids along the edges of our settlements. We can peer at the ant colony with unusual tenderness. Down there, the cupboards may be dirty, the kids may be shouting and the garden in a mess – but such infelicities are shielded from the eye above. Even a retail park or a bungalow begins to look elegant from a mile up. A benevolence descends; a god might love us if that's as close as they got. It isn't easy being us. We're doing our best, going to work in our tiny cars beetling along our miniscule ring roads, trying to earn a living in our mini skyscrapers – before our little lives draw to a close and we're laid to rest in some toy-like cemeteries just visible somewhere by the window's edge.

We can be reassured by how much remains not-us. There's still a lot of empty sky, a lot of sea on which we don't normally sail and a lot of desert in which we haven't found a way to live. Our infernal chatter takes place within a welcome vastness and silence.

We spend far too long pressed dangerously close against our fears and regrets. We have wasted what might be years worrying about catastrophes that haven't yet occurred. Up here, an adequate perspective can be restored. The mountains return to being the molehills they are always likely to have been. It doesn't matter so much who said what to whom at the office, who mislaid the keys or who started the sulk. We'll try not to pull that blind down again in such a hurry; we'll strive to pay a bit more attention to the philosophy of sagehood on offer on the other side.

Window seat in a Club World cabin,
British Airways Boeing 787-8.

A pram in which to be carried
around the world.

The Airline Seat

It's a very restricted place indeed. On some aircraft, it might not allow us more than a few millimetres of movement. If we are lucky, in the favoured parts of a modern cabin, we might be able to stretch out our legs and turn over onto our sides. Yet even the most expensive seat in the house won't be remotely as comfortable as a sofa at home.

Engineers with years of experience have carefully positioned struts and bracing elements across our backs; cloth woven from the hardiest synthetic fibres has been stretched over fire-retardant pads; electric cables have been threaded within precisely milled aluminium sections to provide for light, sound and power; tiny motors have been concealed within footstools and headrests. It's a singular kind of throne on which we are travelling around the planet – and, even when our neighbour begins to snore next to us as we cross over the Andaman Sea, it is a far more stately and elaborate affair than anything on which Charlemagne or Montezuma II ever had the privilege to sit.

The last time we were in anything as cosy and well thought through was, of course, when we lay in a pram – though the connection understandably tends to be downplayed. The chief parallel is that we cannot really move and have abdicated all responsibility. Once we used to lie back on a pillow or a rolled-up blanket and stare up at the passing clouds and the occasional intense face of a well-wisher. There were the rooflines of houses and the flights of seagulls to study. Occasionally we might have been uncomfortable and screamed, but much of the time, we were simply awed by the change of scenery; our horizons had expanded immeasurably since we exchanged the nursery ceiling for this open-air spectacle.

A similarly passive somnolence might descend on us in our airline cot. At first, we might have felt restless and desperate and wondered how we would get through eight hours of this. Now, though, we are a third of the way through and oddly and pleasantly anaesthetised. We're even rather looking forward to the meal. Of course we could get far better things on the ground – bigger plates, fresher portions – but we would have to move and make decisions and it wouldn't be so neatly arranged and intricately planned. Here everything comes automatically, as when we were ill long ago and someone loving came into our room with a tray. There is something reassuring about the uniform, mechanised nature of the offering: the immaculately arranged rectangular plates, the toy cutlery and the chilled, perfectly round bread roll. Down below, we struggle in vain to assert our distinctiveness; up here, we're clearly only 34J and it no longer feels insulting to be so. Why protest at the diminution of our individuality when there are particular pleasures involved, as there are in a care home, a kindergarten or the better kind of prison? It's the sense that others know more clearly than us what we should have, and that we should just cede our will to them. Daddy and Mummy are up at the front, sending news of our flight path on AF13 to Dar es Salaam and Kigali (checking the hydraulic pressure on the EICAS and adjusting the trim), while we quietly eat our crackers and inspect the cheesecake, and try to be good.

We are normally oppressed by options. There are so many places we might go and initiatives we might set into motion; it's never clear that we have done enough. But now we are strapped in and – for a few hours – nothing at all is expected of us. We can do nothing; we can hardly move our heads. It may sound unpleasant, but having very few options and letting others steer us can, in some circumstances, be tantamount to liberation.

Thomas Dworzak, *Stockholm-Lulea
Train, Sweden*, 2017.

We might travel not so much to
reach a destination as to sort out
our minds.

The Train Journey

Ostensibly we might be on a journey to a provincial capital or a coastal town. But really, we're on a journey around unfamiliar and neglected parts of our minds. Wherever the train might happen to be taking us, the incidental – though paramount – benefit of the trip is that it may help us to work out what we think.

Ordinary life goes by far too fast for most of what we have experienced to be adequately processed. There can be enough material in a five-minute exchange with a colleague to power reflections that could last many hours; a 300-page novel could be written in about a half hour inside our minds. Most of the time, we cannot begin to get to grips with the sensations coursing through us; we have no opportunity to notice more than a fraction of what we have lived through. No sooner has one event impacted on us than we are forced to move on to another, yet more turbulent or provocative one.

The inattention can make us ill and sad; we can grow afflicted by a general anxiety because we can't understand what we're specifically scared of. We are weighed down by diffuse sadness because we haven't had the chance to notice what in particular has hurt us. We are irritable with the world because we haven't had the opportunity to shout at one or two people, whose provocations we felt but don't even consciously recall. We grow mentally unwell because we have been denied certain feelings that we are owed. We are foreigners to our own joys; we have not mourned our losses or had the encouragement to analyse our questions. We start to twitch and to wake up at 3 a.m., insomnia being the mind's revenge for all the thoughts we carefully forgot to have in the day. It might have been many months since we were alone with ourselves.

Now, at last, we're on the train – which doubles as a well-disguised machine for self-understanding. We were hoping that the carriage would be empty and we are in luck. There are just a couple of people at the rear; to all intents, we have the place to ourselves. So we take a seat at a window in one of the centre sections, bring out a pad and pen and fall into a reverie. There's no agenda. We're free associating, letting our thoughts come to us as they will, helped along by the rhythmic clicking of the rails and the passing views onto fields and forests.

Thinking is so hard because we are never far from a risk of stumbling into the clutches of an intensely uncomfortable thought. We might, for example, realise that we should leave our partner, that we are furious with someone we're meant to love or that we need to try to find a different sort of work, though we have invested so much in the existing path. With such disclosures waiting for us, no wonder not-thinking can feel like such a priority; how understandable it is that we lean on opportunities for distraction in order to delay, possibly forever, the necessary moments of reckoning.

Yet the train understands our squeamishness and its toll, and has ingenious ways of assuaging us. If a pattern of thought grows difficult, we can evade its hold by glancing out towards the horizon at a row of trees, a bank of clouds or the path of an electricity line. Then as soon as the anxiety has dissipated, we can instantly pick up our rumination where we left off, always knowing we can pause again if it gets too much. Our attention can hover; we can be both within ourselves and lost in the ever-changing views – and in this condition of suspended presence, our better ideas have the freedom to emerge at last.

After hours of train-thinking, we may feel lightened, understood and purged of our previous anxiety and fear. The train's claims have been too modest; it has not only carried us to our destination, but also led us back to key bits of ourselves.

Alec Soth, *Minneapolis,*
Minnesota, USA, 2017.

A lonely place where we can,
at last, feel we belong.

The Hotel Room

There is a particularly intense kind of loneliness that can descend on us when we're meant to feel like we belong somewhere – but don't. We might be with a partner whose understanding of, and interest in, us doesn't match what we long for in the private and vulnerable corners of our minds. Or we might be with close friends who fail to ask us about ourselves, who talk again and again about their skiing holidays and who withdraw when we try to bring up more sincere topics. This is meant to be our family, so why is there so much distance and so much underlying suspicion? Few questions are more painful.

It may seem as if we would only aggravate the loneliness by coming to certain places: isolated diners late at night, empty service stations in the early hours, bleak railway stations in winter or – as in this case – a sterile synthetic hotel room in a gigantic anonymous hotel on the edge of a city where we know no one.

And yet, paradoxically, so-called lonely places do not have to make us feel lonely. Indeed, their unmistakable alienation renders public, and so more acceptable, sentiments that otherwise reside in us in shame. These places seem to tell us that there is nothing unusual in feeling adrift from friends or family or in having lost our bearings. They rehabilitate sadness through their own desolation. We're not alone in being alone.

In this hotel room, there is no more pretence. The bleakness of existence is con-firmed by the traffic roaring along a motorway far below, the peculiar stain on the bedcover and the sound of someone else's television through the wall. And yet we might develop a strange love for this monk's cell, this place at the end of the world. We don't need to fake our smiles. We are lost and the hotel knows it. It doesn't demand good cheer. Everyone else seems similarly abandoned and forlorn, like the cast of a ghost ship adrift in an icy ocean.

In the hundreds of rooms identical to this one, we won't be the only ones wondering where it all went wrong and longing for someone to understand. Without anyone planning for this, we're a community of sorts.

It is easier to feel at home here than in the home that has let us down. We can find a fellowship of the fallen and of the exiled. Whatever the physical ugliness of this room and this hotel, we sense a psychological welcome, and the lonesomeness speaks to the lost pilgrim inside us. In a place where everyone is an outsider, we can start to feel like we belong.

Stuart Franklin, *Cocktail Bar
at the Sofitel Hotel, Abidjan,
Ivory Coast*, 2004.

A place to overcome shyness
and diffidence.

The Foreign Café

Let's imagine that we are, by nature, shy and have been since childhood. We try hard to avoid unfamiliar situations. We don't go to parties where we know no one. We're awkward around strangers. We blush if we're singled out. Going into shops or conveying our intentions to busy, indifferent officials is a trial. We're always keen to try to get someone else to ask for directions.

But no such diffidence will work here, in the largest city of Côte d'Ivoire on the Gulf of Guinea. No one will pay any attention unless we find our voice. The assumption is that, if it's important, surely we will say so – even if that's never quite the way it has been for us.

It's Mariame's role to change the table-cloths after the breakfast sitting and prepare the room for morning snacks and lunch. She's originally from Bounkani in the northeast and has been working here for six years. She has two children and lives with her uncle in a high-rise in Abobo, an hour away by bus.

We may need to leave home in order to expand our personalities and harness new skills. It won't work to look sheepish and hope to be rescued, now that we're on our own here. We have to gather up our courage and speak – and can stand to make immense discoveries, about ourselves and others, if we do so.

It turns out that Mariame is only too keen to chat; we just had to dare to start. She has a ready laugh and a wry manner. She fetches us a slice of pineapple and coconut cake – though the kitchen is officially shut. She tells us about her brother who is setting up a building company in Koumassi after studying in Germany for two years. She wonders if it's our first visit and what book we're reading. She supports the city's football team, Stella Club d'Adjamé, and loves Miriam Makeba and Beethoven.

It no longer matters how different we look and how distant were our introductions to life. The similarities are, in the end, of far greater significance. This is what the shy person refuses to accept. They are repeatedly fooled by appearances; they make too much of the externals. It's our provincialism of the spirit that a visit to Abidjan (or Trondheim or Amarbayasgalant) has an opportunity to correct. We can learn that we all suffer and long in similar ways, that anyone could be our friend, that we are a single human community, constantly hemmed into small tribes by fear.

The next day, we go back and Mariame is there again. We greet each other like old friends. She mentions that she isn't too bad but her knee is giving her trouble. She's brought along a photo of her little Seydou, recently turned 5, in the green stripes of his favourite local team. The universe has expanded.

Holidays

David Hockney, *Waiter,*
Alexandria, 1963.

The goal should be to notice
everything once more — as if we
were artists or small children.

The First Day

In 1963, the London *Sunday Times* sent the already much-celebrated 26-year-old artist David Hockney to Egypt on an assignment to record the great monuments of antiquity: the pyramids outside Cairo, the temples of Luxor and Karnak and the tombs in the Valley of the Kings. Egypt astonished Hockney and induced in him a state of almost perpetual creativity, where everything seemed to hold a secret, and everything was worthy of investigation and reflection. He sketched on whatever was to hand: old envelopes, hotel-room notepapers and the inside covers of his books. However, what struck him most were not the obvious tourist destinations so much as the details of ordinary Egyptian life: the watch of the man at reception, the sandals of the newspaper seller, the signs for the dry-cleaner and the television repair shop.

On arrival in Alexandria, Hockney sat on the terrace of the Hotel Cecil and not only drew the titular Egyptian waiter, but also carefully documented the label on a bottle of local mineral water from the El Natrun valley and a packet of cigarettes. In its delicacy and observational precision (Hockney knew no Arabic), this astonishing study of a bottle might be an emblem of what it means to be properly attuned to a place – to put aside our usual cares and surrender to the interest and beauty of the world, as a child might, as artists will and as we almost never do.

Generally, we notice almost nothing, but we may make an exception for one particular time and place: *the first day in a new destination*. There and then, for once, we too may be shaken from our customary lethargy. Everything leaps out at us: how peculiar the taxis are, the smells in the street, the sound of passers-by, the clothes of the old. Our eyes open properly, as they last did when we were 2 years old and it took us half an hour to get home from the park because there was so much for us to study on the way.

The state is unlikely to last long. After a few days, we tend to go back to our habitual myopia. But even if we only manage it for a short while, the receptivity of that first day remains a possibility that we should strive to enact more regularly and generously, even in places closer to home. We shouldn't need another continent to start to appreciate the texture of existence. We knew how to do so as a small person, and we might do so again. Artists are, in this context, only the emissaries of an appropriately appreciative relationship to the world of which we are all, in theory, capable.

Our travels have an overwhelming lesson to teach us: that we need, whenever we can, to try to look at our lives – with which it is so easy to get dispirited and about which it is so forgivable to despair – as though we were still in some ways on that hopeful, endlessly fascinating *first day* somewhere else, when even a label on a bottle of water has something important to whisper to us.

Massimo Vitali, *Elafonissi*, 2013.

We have been able to make homes
for ourselves in the darkest, most
northerly regions only at a huge,
often forgotten psychological cost.
We need the sun!

The Sun

We may have been tempted to pretend that we came to this part of the world to commune with the spirit of the ancient Athenian statesman and orator Pericles, or to admire the exquisite statuette of Athena Promachos in the Acropolis museum, or to pay homage to the Temple of Apollo Epicurius at Bassae. The reality is far simpler, and in some quarters, more embarrassing to admit: we have come to get warm; we have come to see the world in a primal blinding light. We have come to worship the sun.

It's been the curse of our civilisation to have managed to create ostensibly comfortable homes for ourselves in regions that only a hardy minority would previously have dared to inhabit. In our fragile beginnings, our species had no option but to cling tightly to the clement equatorial zones, but thanks to our ingenuity, we now have everything we need to survive – apparently in comfort – in the near-total darkness, snowstorms and gales of Rjukan (Norway), Barrow (Alaska) and Oymyakon (Russia). But there is a distinction between surviving and flourishing. We may manage to live in London or Gothenburg all year round, but that does not mean that we are remotely able to thrive in their continual mists and vicious, freezing rains.

It cannot be a coincidence that every ancient culture – from the Achaemenids to the ancient Egyptians, the Mesopotamians to the Mayans – honoured and made offerings to the sun so that it might continue to shine its benevolent, life-giving rays on them. Our contemporary veneration of our star lacks any analogous cultural endorsement or prestige; the common associations are around parasols and cocktails by a pool, rather than – as an Egyptian priest would have emphasised – the maintenance of the world spirit in the indomitable form of the sun god Ra.

Nevertheless, even without an official cult, the sun achieves its work of repair. Out here on the bleached rocks, looking out over a scorched, treeless landscape, we remember another side of ourselves that had been lost in the preceding six months of darkness. This self can be less envious of others, more serene, less concerned with control, readier to accept the unknown, in touch with its own senses. We find new arguments for hope in the brightness; the uninterrupted enveloping warmth hints that we won't, perhaps, need to be so afraid, that we can take a chance to trust and that there may be alternatives to anxiety.

Given all that we know about nastiness and despair, cheerfulness is a phenomenal achievement – and the sun-filled places that occasionally inspire it are bearers of their own hugely significant and, in their way, properly sacred wisdom.

Rob Ball, *South Beach Parade,*
Great Yarmouth, 2018.

Here, at last, we are given a
powerful opportunity to confront
one of the most seismic of all
questions: what do I really enjoy?

The Funfair

Most of the time, our pleasure doesn't even come into it. We have to suffer; we have no option but to earn a living, provide for our dependants and endure difficult days. But then come other occasions – far less frequent in number – when, for a while, nothing is expected of us, when the external obligations cease and we are finally free to seek to satisfy only, or chiefly, ourselves.

This might sound like a blessedly uncomplicated brief, but our moments of release have a habit of ushering in difficulties of their own. What are we in fact supposed to do? Who are we, outside of duty? Where should we go? What do we enjoy?

Collectively, our societies spend a great deal more time thinking about how we should make money than how we might fruitfully spend it. Infinite care is devoted to the accumulation of capital and all its associated disciplines: accountancy, management, law … But when it comes to spending, the suggested manoeuvres incline towards a peculiar uniformity and lack of attunement to the distinctive texture of each of our unique personalities. There is a high chance that, without great care, we may end up buying a trip to Disneyland, a skiing holiday, a mountain bike or a barbecue set.

There might not be anything obviously wrong with such investments, except that they might be fundamentally better suited to someone else – a painful realisation that might not come to us until we're halfway up the Big Thunder Mountain Railroad or in a heap at the bottom of a red run. Each of us was – at the start of our lives – gloriously peculiar. We were all very odd small children way back, with set ideas on the wayward things we wanted to do. Our interests paid little attention to the mainstream: we wanted to tie string round some trees or sew some socks for the guinea pig, we had a collection of seeds we tried to germinate, we drew imaginary worlds, we had our own language. We didn't always favour seven nights all-inclusive in the Balearics.

In their touchingly intense attempts to make us smile, funfairs bring our dilemmas to a head. Their desperation reveals just how elusive happiness can be. We may sense – with mounting conviction and regret – that our joys cannot reliably be delivered by the Magic Mouse rollercoaster or the Loop Fighter, Mickey and Minnie's Runaway Railway or the Haunted Mansion.

We may be forced to acknowledge just how much weirder we are than the mainstream narrative allows us to be. We don't actually enjoy birthdays, we are terrified of Christmas, we hate arcades, we get bored during concerts – not because we are misanthropic (though we are that too, of course) but because we are complicated and knotty people who might be most cheered up by a chance to cry for a while or visit a housing project in Turkmenistan, dredge a lake or assist residents in a hospice.

We can thank funfairs for reminding us – to the smells of candyfloss and the shrieks from the Big Dipper – that having fun is one of the most difficult and grave of all the challenges we ever face.

Simon Roberts, *Malvern Hills,
Worcestershire, 17th May 2008*,
2008.

We may have to go away in order
to come properly together.

The Family Trip

We thought we had come to see a patch of countryside or a temple, a canal or a capital – but what emerges is that these are only incidental and secondary stage-sets that permit a far more complicated and important project to unfold: that of understanding and connecting with the young people that we helped put on the earth. However much we strive to get on in normal surroundings, it's only when we have left home that we are forced out of the roles that silently estrange us, and become a family.

For a start, the family trip shatters the customary hierarchies. It no longer matters who is ostensibly what age. New, unexpected vulnerabilities – and skills – emerge. A father turns out to be surprisingly inept at unmooring the boat and worries intensely about getting splashed in the pool; a small boy knows exactly where to put down the anchor and can dive and swim without a care. A mother who is normally intimidated by nothing blushes when she has to explain what she needs in a foreign pharmacy. A parent might be in charge of twenty adults in an office, but when it comes to trying to find garlic in a market, they are the equal of an intrepid 9-year-old, who leads them firmly by the hand through the crowds.

The trip will be full of inconveniences that, at the time, seem as though they detract from the point of being away. With hindsight, we will see that they were, in reality, the crucial incidents. They were what did the work of humanising us and forcing us to understand and forgive each other. It was, in truth, an advantage that we couldn't find the hotel late at night, that the roundabout was wrongly marked, that the food at the inn was repulsive, that we suffered a two-hour detour and that we found a bathroom with only seconds to spare.

The trip will shake us from our normal assumptions about what matters. Of course, the 2,000-year-old monument is of importance in understanding the development of Indo-European civilisation, but there is something significant, too, in the fascination of an 8-year-old with the honey on sale at the roadside or with the lizard rooted on the wall outside the room. Even if the Byzantine architects did cover a church in gold and turquoise tiles that may have been sourced from Persia, they never had a chance to see the adorable basset hound loitering on the steps of the building. And whatever the appeal of the large abstract entity known as 'Japan' or 'Spain', these will in the end always have to take second place to a hotel breakfast buffet that seized the imagination of our young fellow traveller (there were seven different kinds of pastries and three sorts of juices!) and will be mentioned in a speech at their wedding in twenty-four years' time.

The trip was far from flawless. There were many arguments. There was a lost watch and a damaged toe. We will need a long rest on our return. But amidst the turmoil, something compelling developed, nevertheless: we grew more patient, we looked through others' eyes. We didn't see half of what we had hoped, but we learned about love.

Allan Tannenbaum, *"Disco Sally" at*
Studio 54, NYC, 1978.

It can take serious pa;in before we
learn to dance with true silliness.

The Nightclub

In the late 1970s, an unusual figure became a central fixture in Manhattan's premier nightclub, Studio 54 – normally frequented by celebrities, models, the young and the powerful. Sally Lippman was a retired attorney who had been elected to the New York State Bar in the 1920s and had recently lost her husband. Unwilling to spend her last years in silent loneliness, she bought some tight trousers, high-top sneakers and black leather boots and went out four nights a week, in the process making a number of new friends and earning herself the nickname Disco Sally.

Nightclubs do not have a high reputation as therapeutic places. We associate them with grandstanding, a pressure to impress and a narrow group of initiates who intimidate the unfashionable and the ordinary. Most of us are held back from ever attending by a terror that we might be wearing the wrong clothes, that we might be too old or ugly and that we won't know how to dance – as we put it – 'properly'.

Disco Sally was wise enough not to let any such concerns inhibit her. She had lived long enough, suffered deeply enough and was close enough to death to know otherwise. She didn't want to spend her last years in silence in her apartment and so dared to enquire about nearby clubs. Every culture in history, except for our own, has appreciated the need for all sections of society to gather regularly in order to lose themselves to a rhythmic beat. It's been appreciated that, however rational we might manage to be the majority of the time, if we are to stay truly sane, we need to be given the chance to go mad at well-defined intervals.

However reasonable we may normally try to be, in the right sort of nightclub, we can take a break from logic and dignity and flail our arms and legs with gleeful, demented abandon – perhaps, if we are lucky, with some characters in thongs and cartridge belts too.

We should be sensible enough to let folly have its reign. We generally work so hard to ward off any suggestions that we might be daft, but we should accept that the effort was always likely to be in vain and contrary to the facts. We are, each one of us, thankfully, entirely idiotic, and it is a nightclub that gives us the licence to give visible expression to the madness we have repressed for too long and at too great a cost. We become properly serious when we can acknowledge a role for silliness. We mess around not because we think life is a joke, but precisely because we really know it isn't.

As we dance, we break down the normal barriers between ourselves and others. Whatever separates us in terms of age or background can be overcome. We are all similarly ailing, frightened, vulnerable creatures who long for love and acceptance and are terrified of being excluded and judged. To the sounds of Donna Summer and Gloria Gaynor, we can bathe in an atmosphere of compassion and kindness. We don't need to go to an asylum to explore the split-off parts of our broken minds; we need only – with a gleeful swing of our hips and arms – expunge our agonies on the dance floor.

Deedra Baker, *Items of Comfort*, from
the series 'Sanctum', 2012.

The true wish isn't to see a
different place so much as to gain
insight into a different soul.

The Foreign Bedroom

The desire to travel is closely identified by respectable opinion with the aspiration to explore a place through its culture – that is, to know it through its paintings, sculpture, architecture and, perhaps, at a stretch, its music and its food.

The truth is somewhat more complicated and, in areas, delicate. If the real wish is to absorb the insights and strengths of another culture, these cannot reside only, or even chiefly, in old stones and canvases; they must also be present in the people who live and work among a society's historic artefacts. However dispiriting the concept of sexual tourism, it sits awkwardly close to a theme of sincere significance. The deeper promises of a journey may be as capable of being honoured in a foreign bedroom as they are in a temple or archaeological site; a foreign love affair might be the privileged conduit to the virtues of another land.

Yet nothing in the way that travel is presently arranged helps this idea to take root with dignity. It remains extremely difficult to meet people whose culture has touched us. We may see them coming home from work or chatting animatedly in a supermarket and might wonder, with a degree of pain, what their lives might be like, what is happening behind the apartment windows, what ideas they might have, how much they might have to teach us. We may long to commune not just with mighty figures seven generations back, but also with our contemporaries, who walk through the old medieval streets and around the ancient monuments while fetching groceries or buying printer cartridges.

But if we are fortunate, we might, late one evening, find ourselves being led up some steep stone stairs to a small top-floor apartment, and there delighting not only in the emotional and physical endorsement, but also in the distinctive appearance of the books on the bedside table, the creams in the bathroom and the photos pinned in the kitchen next to some unfamiliar pastes and dried herbs. The following morning, we might feel a particular resonance when our new friend mentions an uncle coming for a wedding from an adjoining island, or a brother returning from military service in the mountains.

It won't appear in any guidebooks and to mention it can be fraught, but the sensitive truth is that a foreign bedroom is as likely to deliver us an education as anything we might lay eyes on in the halls of the national museum.

Robert Polidori, *Italian Painting
1300–1500 Gallery, J. Paul Getty
Museum, Los Angeles*, 1997.

Insight can begin when we admit that
we probably don't really know what
all this is for.

The Museum

It's late at night, when the tourists are gone and the repair work and rehanging begins, that the underlying strangeness of museums comes to the fore. Most of the time, we have little option but to passively agree to the value and importance of what we are shown and to walk obediently around the exhibits, guidebook in hand. But in the silent hours, we can dare to ask a few larger questions.

We may note that a lot of what is now displayed in the pristine galleries once resided in chapels and churches – whose walls were abruptly denuded by art dealers flush with dollars in the late 19th century. The pictures were made by artists who, above anything else, were driven by their faith. They didn't care in any isolated way about the beauty of what they were fashioning; they wished the delicate flowers on the dresses of their divinities and the golden halos over the heads of saints to assist believers in acts of worship. They weren't simply making art to be looked at as part of a history lesson – they wanted it to heal souls. For them, it had a therapeutic function; it was a tool. The Madonna needed to look down with infinitely kind eyes in order to lend her tenderness and understanding to the sad and the lonely. St Peter had to look statuesque and wise so as to convey his encouragement to those ready to give up or act immorally. St Francis had to help us to surrender our envy and hard-heartedness so that the world could grow more pure. These were objects in front of which we were meant to fall down on our knees and beg.

To those entrusted with the works today, and who feel that they love them most, such behaviour would seem close to insanity; a security guard could be counted upon to usher out a beseeching pilgrim at great speed. We are meant to know about art, not use it to cry with.

But we have bought our soberness and disengagement around art at high cost. Our art is no longer able – as it once was – to console us and lend us new perspective at our moments of difficulty. We have not found a way for culture to replace scripture; our museums are our new cathedrals only in terms of their scale and cost rather than the sincerity of their missions.

And yet, if only we allowed it to, art could still play a role in our healing. It remains a resource for our emotional evolution. The Madonnas still offer us their grace; there is still hope and courage in landscapes and portraits; there is guidance on offer in small studies of flowers or in abstract canvases of swirling blues and greens.

Art remains a form of therapy, but we have not allowed the museum to present it to us as such, and thereby we deny it the central place in our hearts that we have accorded it in our public pronouncements. Our contemporary difficulty explaining what art might ultimately be for explains the forlorn look of the sacred works on the gallery walls; they have been transplanted into an alien realm which, while it accords them perfect degrees of humidity, disregards their essential original purpose and intent.

We need museums to help us get better; we should remember to ask of them much the same as we once knew to ask of a basilica or a devotional chapel.

A 14 DAY WALK FROM SEA LEVEL AT RÍUMAR CONTINUING TO THE TOP OF 1104 METRE BENICADELL
ENDING BY THE WATERS EDGE IN ALICANTE SPAIN 16-29 FEBRUARY 2016

ROAD

WALKING AWAY FROM BENICADELL

Hamish Fulton, *Road. Walking Away
from Benicadell, Spain*, 2016.

We should make a far bigger deal
of the trips we have been on.

Places of Memory

Benicadell is the name of a mountain in Spain on the border between Valencia and Alicante, which the English artist Hamish Fulton climbed in February 2016. We know about this principally because Fulton made an enormous work of art, almost 2 metres wide by 1 metre high, to commemorate the ascent. In the course of a long career, Fulton travelled to fifty different corners of the world to walk around, and subsequently made large photographs that record – through sober, haunting black-and-white images overlaid with blocks of formal text – exactly where he went, how long it took him and (often) what was the highest point he reached. In April 2011, he went on a clockwise walk around London's M25 motorway (crossing the River Thames at Kingston); in November the following year, he walked up the (4,971-metre-high) Cerro Jorquencal in Chile and, at the start of his career, in 1977, he took five days to make a hundred-mile circuit around the Outer Hebrides, terminating in the Neolithic stone circle at Callanish.

Why endow such relatively ordinary events with such momentousness? Why assume such a grave tone when climbing a mountain or going around a ring road? We tend to be a lot more restrained about our peregrinations. We may invest heavily in our travels, but once they are over, we put them quietly to one side; we might – at the most – dedicate a few pages in a photo album or use a postcard of the seafront as a bookmark. But we are rarely tempted to create something the size of the living room wall to tell the world that we once went to Prague for a long weekend or took a canal holiday in southwestern France for our 40th.

Hamish Fulton would disagree with our modesty – within which he might also detect a note of complacency. For Fulton, we are in no danger of making too much of our travels; the risk lies in how many experiences we let wash over us, and how often we fail to make any attempt to pin them down in memory or give them substantial weight in the story of our lives. We climb mountains, cross oceans, touch glaciers – and can barely remember doing so only shortly afterwards. Fulton proposes that a trip might be one of the most significant events we ever experience, and that there should be no limit to what it means to us, even if it happened to last only a few days. He implicitly argues that we are not pretentious enough, not grand enough. In the 14th century, it was not uncommon to find on a northern European gravestone an inscription commemorating that the deceased had 'travelled to the Holy Land', signalling in no uncertain terms that the most astonishing thing about someone might be that they had made a trip to Israel. It is unthinkable that we would ever accord such honour to a trip today, outside perhaps of a visit to Mars.

Yet our trips may still deserve to be counted among the signal events of our biographies. Many of them are accompanied by important changes in our thoughts. They have a theoretical power to reorient us profoundly. We might decide – sitting on the beach near Le Havre on a rainy August day – that we have no option but to leave a relationship; it could be during a three-day visit to Switzerland that we concretise a wish to start a new career. At 3.40 p.m. on a November afternoon on a trip to Tenerife, watching our 2-year-old son sleeping in the main square of the little town of Garachico, we might begin to understand love.

The ease with which we can travel has not necessarily served us well. We might not follow Fulton in his art, but we might adopt some of his spirit in associating our journeys more firmly with evolutions in our psyches. The point is never just to travel; it's to be able to return as, and remain, slightly different people.

Ruins

Mojave Air and Space Port,
California, USA, 2015.

Where the future comes to die.

Aeroplane Graveyard

At first glance, it could almost be mistaken for a scene from an ordinary busy international airport – until we realise that something darker and more unusual is afoot. Most of the airliners are on crates; their nose cones have been levered off, the ailerons are missing, the doors have been removed, the engines have been ripped out. This isn't an airport, it's a graveyard, a place where planes come to die when they have grown weary of crossing our stratosphere. Many of their old owners, like ageing actors who can no longer bear to look in the mirror, specify that the logos on their tail fins be painted out, as if an acknowledgement of decrepitude would violate the always youthful promises of technology.

There are representatives from all the continents and the most famous airlines. They have come here from Australia, Germany, Britain and America. Machines that spent their working lives being meticulously cared for by specialist mechanics are, in death, hacked at with chainsaws and diggers. Food-trolley doors, seat belts and upended toilet seats clack in the desert wind, making it sound like a marina in a storm. The oldest planes were new only forty years ago, but high technology dates especially fast; the Parthenon looks younger than they do. Inside the cabins there are outsize Bakelite phones, coils of fat electric cables, bulky boxes on the ceilings where film projectors were once slotted. Some aircraft still sport their Pratt & Whitney JT3D engines, the proud workhorses of the 1970s, which generated a then-remarkable 17,500 pounds of thrust; there was little guessing that a few decades later their successors would, with a fraction of the fuel or noise output, be capable of producing four times as much.

Our ancestors could believe that their achievements had a chance of bearing up against the flow of events. We know that time is remorseless and that nothing will endure. Our buildings, our sense of style, our ideas: all of these will soon enough be anachronisms, and the machines in which we now take inordinate pride will seem no less bathetic than Yorick's skull.

Inside many of the planes, the emergency oxygen masks have dropped down from their overhead compartments. They have done so not in the gruesome accident that may come to mind (the engines are on fire and the emergency slides have been inflated!), but simply through the slow erosion of their spring catches. Perhaps we are always more likely to die like this, without particular drama, without firemen in smoke hoods and foam on the runway, without the comfort of a collective accident and the sympathy of newscasters: just through an insipidly slow process of disintegration.

We have a hard time keeping death in mind. It always seems an unlikely possibility – and the faster we can fly to other continents or magically beam our thoughts around the globe, the less likely it seems. Aeroplane graveyards are where we can travel to witness the death of the future, and, despite all our high-tech gadgets, prepare to greet our own ends with grace.

Massimo Vitali, The Arch of
Constantine, Rome, 2008.

We can never be sure what will
happen to our bones or who might
play football with our skulls.

Roman Ruins

By the time the arch was put up, celebrating Emperor Constantine's military victory in 312 CE, the Roman Empire had already seen the first serious wobbles. There had been a string of disastrous rulers, the granaries were depleted, the legions were being challenged in North Africa and the Germanic tribes were restless on the Rhine. The greatest emperors were long gone. Rome had descended into oligarchical squabbling and decadence. The wealthy were paying slaves to attend the army in place of their sons. A strange new religion was taking hold that preached the virtues of forgiving foes rather than executing them summarily, or selling them into slavery. Nevertheless, there remained reasons to be hopeful. This was the greatest empire the world had ever known; the troops stood guard on the borders as far north as Scotland and as far east as Armenia. Viewed from the Palatine Hill at dusk, Rome was an impressive sight. The Colosseum still staged massive gladiatorial games (the famous naval Battle of Cape Ecnomus had recently been re-created there, the central arena flooded for the purpose); the heads of the empire's enemies were still avidly paraded through the streets; there were still plenty of slaves available in the markets; the best chefs still turned out the most accomplished roasted peacocks and swans' livers. It was to be a full ninety-eight more years until the Visigoths, commanded by the warlord Alaric, would finally smash their way into the city in 410 CE and introduce Rome to the new reality.

The Romans gave us the term 'memento mori' (a warning supposedly whispered by slaves to their commanders to ward off the dangers of hubris), without suspecting that their entire civilisation would eventually become such a thing for the world. Yet nowadays, the active sense of tragedy around the old stones has dissipated. Tourists walk by with relative nonchalance. No one actively mourns the loss of the colonies in Algeria or the destruction of the elegant villas on the Bay of Naples. The assumption is that their time was simply up. By the arch there are ice cream sellers, ticket touts and even some well-mannered actors dressed up as Roman legionaries, offering selfies: the fall of Rome as an endearing comedy.

We cannot seem to hold in mind how closely we are following in exactly their footsteps – and how scary the path should feel. Our empire is as unstable, our values as unmoored. It won't happen for a long while yet. There tends to be a lengthy gap between the early hairline cracks and the cataclysm. But the eventual collapse is certain; the only question surrounds the exact route to it.

Individual life is as imperilled, though a beautiful, egocentric blindness persuades us otherwise. We somehow continue to find the notion of our own deaths implausible even as others fall all around us. We take holiday snaps on the edge of our graves.

If we could witness the eventual fate of every one of our projects, we might laugh darkly. Would anyone who watched the departure of Julius Caesar's army on its way to conquer the Gauls, or Marcus Aurelius addressing his immaculately disciplined soldiers on the Rhine, have had it in their hearts to inform these passionate figures of the eventual fate of their efforts?

It is no use merely going to Rome; we have to understand what Rome means for us and our plans, then set about reforming what remains of our lives in its liberating and usefully terrifying shadow.

Swimming pool at deposed President
Mobutu's private palace, Gbadolite,
Democratic Republic of The Congo,
2015.

Death is especially uninterested
in gated compounds and plans for
the next thousand years.

The Villas of Despots

It used to be the favourite of the three pools in Joseph-Désiré Mobutu's $100 million, 15,000-square-metre palace, on top of a hill above the jungle near the little town of Gbadolite in the north of what was once Zaire (now the Democratic Republic of the Congo). There was a complicated water slide and a golden jacuzzi. Servants would circulate with the dictator's favourite oysters and Belgian mussels, while the local village lacked electricity. He had a ready smile when he was in a good mood and cages full of wild animals for when he was not. He had a 32,000-metre airstrip built in the vicinity and hired Air France's Concorde to go to Paris on shopping trips with his wives (the first of whom was called Marie-Antoinette). He had twenty-one children and explained proudly that he had slept with a thousand Zairean virgins. During his presidency he stole $15 billion from the central bank and – while things were good – found a lot of friends, among them Pope John Paul II, the Director of the CIA, Richard Nixon, George Bush and Valéry Giscard d'Estaing. For his 55th birthday party, the renowned pastry chef Gaston Lenôtre flew in (on Concorde) from Paris with a large chocolate cake.

Then, naturally, things fell apart for Mobutu. There was unrest in the south, the TV station was seized and the population rose up. After a scramble to find a jet large enough for the luggage, there was exile and an ignominious end in a small apartment in Morocco. The villa was ransacked and the Italian marble stripped. The palace's thousand staff were sacked; a few of the more enterprising ones now offer tours to curious visitors. The jungle will soon have finished reclaiming the staterooms.

It is those who strive hardest to defy oblivion who have a particular habit of ending up humiliated by its march. Mobutu was the Pharaoh Amenhotep III of his time. Amenhotep was an African dictator, who in the 14th century BCE had himself sculpted out of blocks of quartzite sandstone and positioned outside a monumental gateway of the Temple of Karnak at Luxor, where he remains, smashed and eroded by time, staring out solemnly into an eternity with other things on its mind.

It's almost tempting to imagine a less ignominious fate for Mobutu, the man who called himself The All Powerful. Most of us somewhere, deep down, have our fantasies of luxurious palaces and world domination; every small child is a little emperor. It can be almost thrilling when the baddie gets away with it. This one just overplayed his cards: every road outside the capital was left unpaved, and the only surgeons in the country were his own. Once Concorde came in with just a crate of oysters for lunch. It was always going to end badly.

Knowing how the grandest projects conclude shouldn't empty everything of meaning. But it should put us especially on guard against all that smacks of pride. (It's the four stone lions from Italy in the villa's entrance hall that now look most pitiful.) Modesty has the best chance against fate; time reserves its pitiless laughter for those who want things to last and stamp their feet so that everyone will take them seriously. The jungle ruins have much to say even to those of us with ostensibly more modest ambitions; if the site were only more accessible, it should be a favoured destination for all those who nurse – and are exhausted by – hopes of grand destinies. Let us live in such a way that time will not laugh too much at our plans.

Ornithomimidae skeleton, Central
Museum of Mongolian Dinosaurs,
Ulaanbaatar, Mongolia.

Ancient ornithomimids politely
renewing our sense of our own
absurdity.

Central Museum of Mongolian Dinosaurs

They got into a fight one day, 83 million years ago, on a bleak ridge in what is now the Gobi Desert, 600 kilometres south of the Mongolian capital Ulaanbaatar – which was then part of a lush forest teeming with *Therizinosaurus*, *Ankylosaurus* and *Velociraptor* and echoing at night to the martial cries of *Protoceratops* and armoured *Tsagantegia*. It's unclear what got them into their conflict. Perhaps they were arguing over a nest of flavoursome *Quaesitosaurus* eggs, or both had their eyes on an identical baby *Nemegtosaurus*. Whatever the dispute, it proved to be the end for both of them; they took bites out of each other's thin necks with their sharp toothless beaks and then fell into a mortal tangle, their bodies disappearing into the sandy ground until their discovery – by an all-female team of Polish palaeontologists from Warsaw – in the early 1970s.

Today they have pride of place in the main hall of the Central Museum of Mongolian Dinosaurs (formerly the Lenin Museum) in central Ulaanbaatar. Beside them stands a perfectly intact skeleton of a *Tarbosaurus bataar*, the Asiatic twin of the more famous *Tyrannosaurus rex*, as well as a full skeleton of an *Oviraptor*, known for its unusually large brain and tenderness towards its children (they have been found hunched protectively over nests full of eggs).

Mongolia's desert floor is a graveyard filled with the corpses of *Achillobator* and *Udanoceratops*, *Pinacosaurus* and *Erketu*. None of these were a brief presence; they collectively thrived in the region for 79 million years (between 145 and 66 million years ago), until the disastrous day more coldly known in science as the K–Pg extinction event, when an asteroid 10 kilometres wide slammed into the Gulf of Mexico and brought matters to a sharp close.

Our brains aren't well suited to holding on to the idea of how precariously positioned our species is; we assume things to be more or less solid. We're not expecting anything to fly in from outer space. We think it's an achievement that we date back 200,000 years. Those 6-metre-long *Gallimimus* combatants in the Ulaanbaatar museum held out for 17 million years, yet still they have gone. There have been five mass extinctions since the earth began. Five times, a majority of living things have been wiped out and most of complex life has had to begin anew. Any sober assessment of our future has to acknowledge the unlikelihood that we will make it in the long term.

Sooner than we might think, we will be dug out of the earth and shown off in an exhibit – and may appear as puzzling and as incidentally sweet to our successors as the parrot-beaked *Psittacosaurus* and speedy little *Mononykus* seem to us.

The Ulaanbaatar museum isn't trying to make us give up; yet it might well encourage us to approach ourselves and our squabbles with a little more generosity of spirit and lightness of heart, underpinned by an awareness of how ridiculously and inconsequentially brief it will all be.

Museum looted by ISIS in Palmyra,
Syria, 2015.

One of the more conclusive
arguments - were we to need any -
against our species.

Palmyra

If we ever needed reasons to give up on the human race, we could do worse than begin with the 14th May 2015, the date when soldiers belonging to the Islamic State – supposedly driven by a desire to set up a caliphate, but in reality suffering from a particular kind of mental illness – overran Syrian government forces and took hold of the archaeological site of Palmyra, in south-central Syria, 210 kilometres northeast of Damascus.

The city had once, long ago, been one of the most elegant and powerful in the world. At its zenith in the 3rd century CE, it was known for its colonnades, its theatres, its solid granite public baths, its bronze statues of local aristocrats and gods and its military prowess under the Palmyrene King Odaenathus (who invaded Egypt and routed the armies of the Persian Emperor Shapur I). Palmyra endured far longer than the American Empire; it thrived for many centuries more than modern Manhattan. Then, gradually, the trade routes on which it depended shifted course and it fell into decline, until it was finally wrecked in the early 15th century by a marauding tribe from Uzbekistan.

Palmyra did not disappear from the map, however. It became a famous archaeological site, attracting European visitors who enjoyed its melancholy atmosphere, sketched the remains of its temples and wrote poems to its past glories. A museum was set up to house a considerable collection of deities, statues and funerary monuments.

Though the place was already a ruin, it was not ruined enough for the tastes of the soldiers of the Islamic State. They wanted to finish off what the marauding Uzbek tribe had begun. So they tracked down the chief archaeologist, Khaled al-Asaad, a gentle and learned man with a worldwide reputation in his field and many books to his name and who had been in charge of the site for the previous thirty years. They asked him for a full tour, took a careful note of where everything was and then, though a distraught Khaled begged them to stop, blew up the statue of the Lion of Al-lāt, fired mortars into the 1st-century Temple of Baalshamin and the Monumental Arch, dynamited the Temple of Bel, destroyed the 2nd-century Tower of Elahbel, pulverised the ancient tombs of Iamliku and Atenaten, ransacked the museum, smashed every display case and desecrated every female statue they could find – then, having made sure he had seen all their handiwork, they cut Khaled's head off with a sword and hung his body feet first from a column in the main avenue.

Palmyra is now one of the saddest places in the world. It's where we should come to properly despair of who we are. It's no longer telling us the story of an ancient Semitic city. It's a monument to the madness in each of us. Despite our sentimental stories, despite how sweet we can be when we look after small children, despite our shiny spaceships and impressive phones, we belong to one of the most murderous, cruel, savage and pitiless life forms that have ever dwelt on the earth. With Palmyra's example, it may be best to settle this matter of our worth once and for all; thereafter, a lot less will still have the power to surprise and appal us.

Paige Lipsky, *Calvary Cemetery,
Queens, with the Manhattan Skyline*,
2017.

The dead of Queens providing
protection from the living of
Manhattan.

Calvary Cemetery

Behind the cemetery are some of the most driven, clever, productive, ruthless and cynical people ever to have been gathered into a single space in the history of humankind. On the island of Manhattan, we don't exist beyond the money and fame we accrue; there is no friendship or pity; everyone is longing to see everyone else disgraced; people are proud of their cynicism; we need to triumph rapidly or leave town.

It's to defend ourselves against the fear and panic induced by this terrifying piece of real estate that we should take a subway out to Calvary Cemetery in Queens: 365 acres tightly filled with the bodies of military heroes, Wall Street titans, Fifth Avenue princesses and the ordinary heart attack and cancer victims of the northeastern United States. It might sound sad to spend a few hours communing with the dead in this way, but it may – in these parts – be a great deal more reviving than attempting to connect with the living. Amidst the graves, there is at least room for sympathy; there is space for thoughtfulness and tenderness; no one mentions an IPO.

Everyone – whatever their wealth – slips into a similar-sized coffin. The most famous and awe-inspiring are reliably forgotten within two generations, and every corpse, however large its last tax return, is quickly gnawed at by similar armies of undiscriminating worms. Death is beautifully democratic; to microbiotic life, the Upper East Side tastes much the same as the Bronx. The former leave exclusive penthouses on Park Avenue feet first in the morning and, by evening, are interred for eternity in a plot no larger than one of their former bathtubs. Everyone is silent; there is no more gossip; the journalists have gone; the invitations dry up.

The largest cities of modernity excel in their power to shatter our sincerity and peace of mind. It becomes impossible not to worry that we have been excluded, and not to wake up from nightmares about our downfalls. We know that we should leave time for introspection, creativity and vulnerable conversation, but we are too scared to remember how to begin. We forget all that is gentle and touching and that we understood so well when we were 5. We cannot turn away from a media which appals us with news of never-ending threats to our reputations and livelihoods. We know we can never be loved outside of what we can boast about at dinner.

The cemetery cares nothing for all of this. It bids us to sit on a bench and commune for a while with its stable and heartfelt verities. It asks us to live in such a way that we do not dishonour ourselves from the perspective of death. We should worry only about those things that still seem serious when contemplated from the far side of the grave. We should measure our thoughts against the implied verdicts of a skeleton.

We can be grateful for the dead of Queens for trying to save us from the living of Manhattan.

The Sublime

Albert Bierstadt, *Among the
Sierra Nevada, California*, 1868.

The pleasures of being made
to feel small.

The Sierra Nevada

The painting itself was vast, and the scene it depicted even more so. After the German-American artist Albert Bierstadt completed it in 1868, he toured it around Europe, placed a velvet curtain around it and sold tickets so people could view it in fifteen-minute time slots. It won a gold medal from the Academy in Berlin and, after intense bidding, was bought by one of the richest men in America, Alvin Adams, founder of Adams Express, the world's first high-speed door-to-door courier service. It depicts, with a few liberties, a spot at the base of the tallest mountain in the United States, the 4,421-metre-high Mount Whitney in east-central California on the border of the Sequoia National Park, which Bierstadt first visited in 1863. The prolific Bierstadt made five further trips around the west, all of them sponsored by railroad companies that hoped to garner interest through artistic representations of the regions they served. It was said by one critic at the time that half of those heading out west had, whether they knew it or not, been encouraged to move by a Bierstadt painting.

Being made to feel small is not, in general, a pleasant experience. We bristle at being reduced in importance at the hands of a haughty waiter or indifferent colleague. We strive to assert ourselves among our acquaintances and boost our standing through achievement. Nevertheless, in the 18th century, the Anglo-Irish philosopher Edmund Burke identified a different, more pleasant sensation of smallness that we might experience in front of the mighty manifestations of nature: glaciers, oceans, mountains, the night sky. Before an eternally snow-capped mountain, far from feeling humiliated at our minuteness, we might be enhanced and uplifted; we might no longer care so much about the competitive jostling in the cities; it might not be such a worry any more who was earning what and who had been spoken of well at parties. Burke termed this redemptive sensation of smallness 'the sublime' and it was largely thanks to him that a new sublime-seeking tourism arose. People actively set out to find places that could reduce them in size in their own imaginations. Mountains and waterfalls that might have been ignored previously became a focus for tourists seeking solace from their unquenched ambitions and frustrated sense of importance.

Bierstadt's painting is ostensibly of Mount Whitney, but it is at the same time about our feelings towards our brother-in-law and about a new Bay Area technology company we have read about in a breathless article. We need vast scenes and the places they depict more than ever, not just for our physical health, but to help us contain the impatient questions inside our tormented minds: a 10-million-year-old mountain created by the pressures on the intermontane west has developed a critical role in dampening our unwarranted and poignant frenzy that we do not matter enough.

Aerial view of Meteor (Barringer)
Crater, Arizona, USA.

Much of us is made of star dust.

Meteor Crater

Day to day, the evidence for the idea is so slight, and the entire concept so peculiar and contrary to our sense of things, that it is no wonder that we push it to the back of our minds and have resisted giving it its due place in public consciousness. And yet the evidence is incontrovertible: much of who we are and of how life on the planet has taken hold is to be explained by the arrival of asteroids and comets.

In the Earth's early days, 4.5 billion years ago, things were entirely dry, lifeless and inert until – around 3.8 billion years ago – the planet underwent what is known as the Late Heavy Bombardment. In this roughly 100-million-year period, giant planets were knocked off their normal orbits and scattered objects into the path of the terrestrial planets. A hundred thousand or so asteroids and comets of all different sizes smashed into the atmosphere-less Earth, and on board these extraterrestrial objects came the central ingredients for life: the water in the oceans, the calcium in our teeth, the potassium in our brains, the carbon in our hair, the glycine in our cells and the ribose in our DNA.

The evidence has – since then – been well concealed. We can see the pockmarked surface of the Moon or Mars well enough through our telescopes, but on Earth, the mantle of life has cleverly disguised the story of our origins. Most of the craters have been filled in by vegetation, water or erosion. There remain only a hundred or so pristine impact sites to be seen anywhere on the planet.

For a long time, the locals refused to accept that this was what the place could be. They took it to be a volcano; many just called it a mountain. But one local meteoriticist, Harvey Nininger, insisted on the extraterrestrial theory. He toured the area, picking up small fragments of the alleged meteorite; he wrote a book called *A Comet Strikes the Earth* and set up the American Meteorite Museum not far from the crater's rim. Settled scientific opinion now agrees: the big hole in the ground exists because, 50,000 years ago during the Pleistocene epoch, a nickel–iron meteorite 50 metres wide slammed into Arizona at 12.8 kilometres a second, releasing approximately as much energy as 10 megatonnes of TNT.

Fortunately, it's one of the most photogenic of all craters and so we might choose to pin an image of it to the fridge door and turn to it whenever we feel any temptations towards self-righteousness or grandiosity. If we were founding a new religion dedicated to wisdom and maturity, the crater might have a good claim to be considered the new Jerusalem.

Huang Gongwang, *Dwelling in the Fuchun Mountains* (detail), 1350.

Wherever we actually live, we can maintain a hut in the mountains of the mind.

The Fuchun Mountains

The Fuchun Mountains belong to a modest range – most peaks rise to only 1,000 metres – that runs southwest of Hangzhou, along the northern bank of the Fuchun River in southern China. They are exceptionally beautiful peaks, dotted with pine trees and alpine grasslands, often coated in mist in the early mornings and largely deserted.

Though China has been an unusually urban society since the 10th century, in its art, it has looked constantly to the countryside. In its most favoured landscape scrolls, one theme has been recurrent: the idea of a small wooden hut set somewhere beneath some trees in a highly remote location with a view onto mountains. In one of the most famous of these works, by the 14th-century artist Huang Gongwang, ink and brush strokes conjure up a beguiling world suggestive of harmony with nature and peace with ourselves.

Yuan and Ming Dynasty China were not societies in which inner calm was ever particularly easy to claim. There was a huge expansion in trade but wealth was unequally distributed, the court in Beijing was filled with intrigue, careers could be quickly made but as rapidly undone, rumours could destroy reputations forever and there was ceaseless manoeuvring for favours and advancement. However high an individual might have risen, it was impossible to be sure that they would not lose it all at any moment.

In the circumstances, many of the most ambitious members of society developed a veneration for the concept of – when the time called for it – surrendering all worldly goals and taking to a hut in the mountains. There, a person might spend the rest of their life painting, studying Buddhism, writing poetry and eating and dressing with utter simplicity. There was a respect for what were called *yinshi* (hidden men), *yimin* (disengaged people) or *chushi* (scholars at home), honourable terms for those who had dropped out of the competitive race in the name of freedom from anxiety and fulfilment of the soul.

It was no coincidence that these Chinese recluses went to the mountains. Most people resided on the plains and in the cities, so mountain land was cheap to buy; it was possible to survive on a fraction of what life in Nanjing or Ningbo would cost. More importantly, mountains directed the mind appropriately. Through their height, their isolation, their untouched dignity, they symbolised the virtues of an independent life, no longer in hock to political factions and the whims of urban opinion. It didn't matter so much what the Emperor's favourites were doing when the day could be spent contemplating the dissolution of the ego in a Buddhist text, going out to pick some mushrooms and berries for dinner and looking at the sun setting behind a pine forest.

The Gap lookout, Watsons Bay,
Sydney, New South Wales, Australia.

A life well lived is one in which
we properly consider the temptations
of jumping ... before returning
safely home.

The Gap Cliff

There were – until very recently – no barriers. The 30-metre drop onto rocks makes death a certainty. The cliff is a twenty-minute drive from the centre of Sydney. It's extremely beautiful, too, formed about 150 million years ago during the Jurassic era when a large chunk of sandstone cracked and started to be eroded. Silver gulls wheel languidly around the base and a variety of eucalypts decorate the upper ridge. Around a hundred people jump off the top every year; many more come by and think very seriously about it.

Our societies are especially sensitive on the topic of suicide. For the ancient Romans, a prerequisite of a good life was the knowledge that it could be ended at any time, were it to grow unbearable. If mortal illness threatened, or if a person had been gravely disgraced or was being persecuted by enemies, then Rome's Stoic philosophers did not insist on the necessity to keep going. Unlike later Christian thinkers, they posited no responsibility to a god or to the state. Everyone's life was in the end their own, to do with as they wished.

Few Roman thinkers did, in fact, commit suicide, but what mattered for them was not so much the actual event as its possibility. It was the thought of death that was being – intelligently and judiciously – invited to lend relief for the troubles of life. 'The wise man will live as long as he ought, not as long as he can,' wrote Seneca. 'He always reflects concerning the quality, and not the quantity, of his life. As soon as there are numerous events in his life that give him trouble and disturb his peace of mind, he can set himself free.' Seneca was not advocating random or thoughtless exits; he was attempting to give us more courage in the face of anxiety by reminding us that it is always within our remit, if we have genuinely tried everything and the pain is beyond our capacities, to choose a noble path out of our troubles. He was seeking to strip willed death of its associations with pathology and to render it instead an option that the wise would always know was there as a backstop. It wouldn't even need to be a grim spectre; the Stoics emphasised that death could be a moment to celebrate what had gone well in a life, to thank friends and to appreciate the beautiful sides of the world. The idea was to see death as a door through which we knew we had the right and the power to walk if it felt necessary.

The Gap is not a cliff to die from; it's a place to focus on why life matters. It's a sublime location in which to accept that life should be a willed act, not a duty. It's a place to ask ourselves, with every possibility of an end before us, why we might, after all, keep going. It may take a serious confrontation with the idea of death for us to finally ascertain what might make life properly worthwhile for us.

As importantly, the Gap has become a place of friendship. Before his death in 2012, a local resident called Don Ritchie, a retired World War II veteran, went out daily onto the cliff to engage with people who might have been tempted to jump. The 'Angel of the Gap', as he became known, would start by asking: 'Can I help you in some way?' and then would gradually build up to a connection and a friendship. His view was that almost everyone who thinks of killing themselves is essentially short of a friend. We die from isolation, not of our troubles. Since Ritchie's passing, his work has been carried out by a new generation of volunteers.

The Gap isn't a place for suicide, it's a place to work out a better way to live.

Agriculture

Zebras migrating, Chobe National
Park, Botswana.

We might take inspiration from
an animal that has resisted every
attempt to tame it.

Chobe National Park

The best time and place to come and see them in their thousands is during the rainy season, as they travel between the Chobe River floodplains in Namibia and the grasslands of Botswana's Makgadikgadi region 500 kilometres away. Their stripes are every bit as astonishing as they seemed when we were children, defying us to believe that they have not been patiently painted on by a skilled artist. Each example has a thick dorsal line running from the forehead to the tail, and branching stripes running downwards along the body, except for where they arch and split over the front and rear legs. Every backside has its unique pattern, allowing their young to find their mother in the herd, while the collective shimmering of the lines confuses their most feared predators, the colour-blind lion and hyena, as well as providing protection from horseflies, which appear averse to landing on such complicated decoration. Zebras may share a common ancestry and profile with horses, but they have none of the horse's docility or desire to help us out – a factor which has changed history. It isn't as if we haven't tried to get them to pull our ploughs or carry our luggage. Every effort, however, has been comedically unsuccessful. In 1261, Sultan Baibars of Egypt sent a zebra to Alfonso X of Castile, which promptly threw the king off its back. In 1471, a zebra gifted by a Somalian king to the emperor of China grew so unruly it had to be put down. The Germans tried to create a mounted zebra division in Namibia and lost ten men in the process. And in the late 19th century, the eccentric zoologist Walter Rothschild tied six of them to a carriage and attempted to drive to Buckingham Palace, but they broke free and escaped across the Hampshire countryside.

Of all the 148 larger terrestrial herbivores, humans have only ever managed to domesticate five kinds: sheep, goats, cows (including oxen), pigs and horses. And we've had moderate local success with ten others: Arabian one-humped camels, Bactrian two-humped camels, llamas, alpacas, donkeys, reindeer, water buffalo, Bali cattle, mithans and yaks. Crucially, not a single one of these fifteen was native to North America, Australia or sub-Saharan Africa, while South America had to make do with llamas and alpacas, which are not much good with ploughs and collapse quite easily when anyone tries to ride them. So the big, useful animals existed overwhelmingly only in Eurasia, and this is the single greatest reason why Eurasian societies were able to develop a great deal faster than others, and hence why some ended up colonised and others colonists. Without an animal to pull a plough and carry heavy things, there was – until the invention of steam power – a strict limit to possible development.

It turns out, therefore, that the zebra's refusal to help out humans was more or less directly responsible for the relative economic impoverishment of the regions in which it dwelt. We can, from a certain perspective, almost admire the zebra for its steadfastness; whatever the inducements, it was not going to make friends with us or tie its fate to our whims. Each one of us submits to so much, and often for no good reason, that we might take inspiration from this animal's stubborn independence of mind. Zebras injure more zookeepers per year than tigers. They are impossible to lasso with a rope and have still never been successfully ridden any distance. There is a zebra inside each of us that might sometimes learn to resist sugar cubes and do more of its own thing.

Wheat harvest, Southern
Saskatchewan, Canada.

Some of our troubles begin here.

Saskatchewan

Wheat has, by most accounts, been an astonishing success for our species and a particular triumph for Canada. Half of the 35 million tonnes of wheat the country grows every year (it's the earth's fifth largest producer) is harvested in Saskatchewan, and most of that is grown in the bottom third of the province. If 1 tonne of wheat makes 1,700 loaves of white bread, a great many of the world's slices of toast will have originated in these parts. Head out from Regina, the provincial capital, in late August or early September and the horizon will be dotted with rows of gigantic John Deere S690s and New Holland CR10s cutting their way through vast prairie lands carpeted with the heavy blonde stalks of the most fecund grass the planet has ever known.

We've only been doing this for a – relatively – short while. *Homo sapiens* goes back 200,000 years, but it was only around 9,500 BCE in southeastern Turkey that we started wheat cultivation. The story is usually told as one of triumph: our pre-agricultural ancestors were both starving and stupid, and only thanks to the discovery of agriculture did we gain food security and the freedom to use our leisure to develop writing, mathematics and large cities with public baths. No longer did we need to get on our knees and forage under myrtle berry bushes; we could wait for a loaf to be brought to the table and read Thucydides instead.

It's an inspiring story, but not necessarily a wholly accurate one. From many perspectives, the agricultural revolution was a disaster from which we are still trying to recover. While our food supply grew in absolute terms, it also became less diverse and more vulnerable to disease; in bad years, there was a great deal more malnutrition and starvation than there had ever been. *Homo sapiens* grew less healthy (and shorter) the more fields we cultivated. With people now settled in villages, population numbers exploded, wiping out the original gains in productivity and creating a need to labour ever harder to feed new mouths. Work grew more boring and repetitive. Hunter-gatherer societies had exercised their minds on a wide variety of challenges, searching for honey one day, tracking a deer the next; now it was always the same back-breaking task. There was increased inequality too: a few managed to seize valuable lands, and edged out and enslaved the others. Having lived for most of our history in bands of no more than a hundred, with a spirit of equality and a powerful sense of community, we were now herded by people who declared themselves kings into groups of thousands and soon millions. There was an increase in free time for some – but humans are not necessarily very good at handling empty hours. It helps to have a sharply focused mission (to climb a pear tree or track down a wild turkey). We grew bored and anxious; our thoughts tormented us and we wondered in vain what we might be for. To appease our alienation, we began eating too much.

We're prone to explain our psychological dissatisfactions in too narrow a way. We need to investigate broader swathes of history to explain some of our sorrows. It isn't just our parents who have made us sad; some of the blame belongs squarely with those golden wheat fields of southern Canada.

Rice terraces at sunset, Maruyama
Senmaida, Kumano-shi, Mie Prefecture,
Japan.

To change the way we think might
require us to alter how we work.

Maruyama Senmaida

They've been growing rice in this part of central Japan for 3,000 years; it has always been a complicated business and remains so to this day. Seeds will only germinate properly if they've been sitting for many months in a sunlit pool of water at least 5 centimetres deep, but the stalks can only be harvested when the water has been drained and they have been able to dry out for a few weeks. This makes for an unholy degree of complication. It means that rice generally has to be grown in terraces facing the sun, with water flowing down the hillside through a well-managed network of sluices and dykes. There has to be an upper terrace that functions as a reservoir or holding pond – and an extremely detailed agreement between all the farmers as to when their particular terrace will be ready to receive or be drained of water. The whole community needs a firm grasp of hydrodynamics, a law-abiding nature and a highly punctual and disciplined outlook.

When trying to understand the particularities of the Japanese character, sociologists in the 20th century focused on what has come to be known as 'the rice theory', which states that a nation whose diet has for centuries depended on rice will develop many of the qualities that are necessary for its successful cultivation. They proposed that the Japanese are the way they are – thorough, collaborative, precise, traditional, focused on the 'we' rather than the 'I' – principally because of the virtues a majority of them had to exercise to bring in the harvest; the rice terraces of places like Maruyama Senmaida moulded the national character. Conversely, the same sociologists have proposed that the characteristics of many Western nations – individualistic, impatient, self-reliant and innovative – have been the consequence of their cultivation of a very different plant: wheat.

However fanciful the two theories might sound, they point us to the idea that, far more than we're normally prepared to recognise, our jobs don't just occupy our energies, they also shape our personalities. Teaching children all day will give us one sort of temperament, designing advertising campaigns another. Politicians might speak one way over the dinner table, psychotherapists another.

This can open up an avenue for compassion. The regrettable awfulness of many people won't necessarily always be their fault; it may be a function of the work they have found themselves doing. If people in television are often disloyal, paranoid, unreliable and insincere, this may have far more to do with the vagaries of their industry than of anything fixed in their natures. If we gave them a rice field to cultivate in a picturesque village south of Osaka, some water sluices to manage and some neighbours to depend on, they might in time grow exceptionally calm, collaborative and forbearing.

Similarly, at a state level, the atmosphere of many modern nations – their ruthlessness, immaturity, aggression and exhibitionism – may ultimately be a function of the way most of their citizens have to earn their living rather than of any drastic deterioration in human nature. Japan's rice theory asks us to explain, and then perhaps one day reform, our characters by looking into an unfamiliar and often painful place: at who our jobs ask us to be every day.

Lemon trees, Pedalino, Sicily, Italy.

The sacred fruit of a new religion
in a better world.

Pedalino

Ideally, we would agree to live only where lemon trees grow, a favoured zone between the 40° parallel in the north and the 40° parallel in the south, which includes California, Uruguay, South Africa, Italy, Spain and Greece. The trees have intuitively put their roots on certain of the ideal ingredients for fulfilment. They need nine hours a day of sunshine, a temperature of between 20° and 25° Celsius, little wind, protection from frosts, a good amount of room from their neighbours and occasional gentle pruning. Under such conditions, they will – from their fourth year on – reliably produce some sixty lemons a tree for thirty years.

Here in Sicily, it will be the Siracusa or *femminello* lemon, the skin of which is particularly delicate and flavoured and which can be eaten whole. The lemon was said to have been brought to Sicily by the Arab Emir Ibrahim II early in the 10th century, having first been grown in Assam in northeast India. It has sunk deep into Sicilian culture. Its relief is sculpted in several churches on the island, it has had songs dedicated to it and it has acquired a saint, St Lucia – and special powers of revenge. (Supposedly it's possible to make an enemy fall ill by taking a lemon to Mass, sticking pins in it and throwing it into a well.) It anchors a range of recipes – Sicilian lemon cake, lemon marinade, lemon pappardelle, granita, *salmoriglio* – but it works as well squeezed into some cold water or directly onto the tongue.

As usefully, it is an object for contemplation. It's a perfect symbol of hope. It has condensed the hours of sunshine it has grown in and beams these back to us, even in midwinter, from a window ledge or a bowl, in a way that can alleviate our dejected moods and remind us of reasons to endure. The lemon understands pain well enough. It isn't a cosseted and overly delicate fruit. It grows in hard rocky soil, its skin is somewhat mottled and its shape irregular, but it insists on cheerfulness nevertheless. Its yellow is always vivid, and its taste reliably vibrant and tart.

It's easy for an attitude of hope to fall under suspicion. It can seem close to naïvety. Sadness and alarm can seem the more grown-up and prestigious options. But after we have cried all we need to, and spent a good deal of time under the covers, hope reasserts its importance. It is what we need to rely on to return once again to fractured relationships, frustrated business plans or unsatisfactory families.

To walk along the rows of a Sicilian lemon orchard on a clear morning, catching the combined scents of thousands of fruit, can be enough to challenge even the most entrenched melancholy. Of course much has gone wrong; it always does (though we too seldom have an appropriate grasp of just how widespread difficulties are in every life), but there remain small pockets of beauty and kindness. The lemon is our mind's ally in its never-finished quest to ward off tides of despair. It is the guardian of confidence and trust. In a perfect religion, the lemon would be the chief sacred object, deified and often in view, reminding us of life's potential; an imaginary repository for all that we too often lose sight of in our moods of fear and exhaustion.

Infrastructure

Salginatobel Bridge, Schiers,
Switzerland, built 1930.

A model of how technology and nature
might co-exist - and of how a thing
(or a person) might be at once gentle
and strong.

Salginatobel Bridge

The Salginatobel Bridge is a 133-metre-long reinforced-concrete span that connects the villages of Schiers and Schuders in the canton of Graubünden in eastern Switzerland. It was designed in 1929 by the 57-year-old Swiss engineer Robert Maillart and carries a road over a 90-metre gorge through which runs the Salgina Brook and around which golden eagles circle, on the lookout for squirrels and marmots below.

Until the 20th century, all bridges that our species ever made relied on stone, wood or steel, but Maillart found a way of using concrete to convey an impression of lightness and ease even as his three-hinged arch bridge hangs over a precipitous drop.

The bridge models for us how we might be both powerful and tender. It can carry a procession of school buses or tanks on its back in safety; it can function uncomplainingly through the deepest winter snows, in the heaviest downpours and when the wind is howling along the valley. But it understands how not to make a fuss: it discreetly avoids letting on how difficult its task really is. If this were a person, it wouldn't let its partner know all the strenuous things it sometimes does for them. It wouldn't sigh and explain: *I listen to you when I'm slightly bored; I got your sister a nice present at Christmas, even though I find her irritating; I agreed to go camping, though it's my least favourite kind of holiday; I can't stand the pile of newspapers and magazines you keep on the kitchen table, but I don't clear them away because I know you like having them there.* It would undertake the labours of love without letting the loved one know the efforts it had made: it might not admit how many times it had stayed up late worrying or had cried itself to sleep with frustration. It says less than it needs to.

The bridge is an emblem of how technology can intervene in the natural world without destroying it. A human creation need not always ruin the landscape it sits in. The grandeur of the gorge is enhanced, not wrecked, by Maillart's bridge; its elegance joins with what we love in the ancient pine trees and the steep rocks of the sides and the cascades of the stream.

The underlying feat of the Salginatobel Bridge isn't to link a couple of alpine villages; it's to help us feel proud of ourselves. Here is massive strength that can leap like an ibex over a gorge or can carry us on its shoulders like a loving parent bearing a child over a swollen river. The human stamp, even on a large scale, can sometimes show off what is best in us.

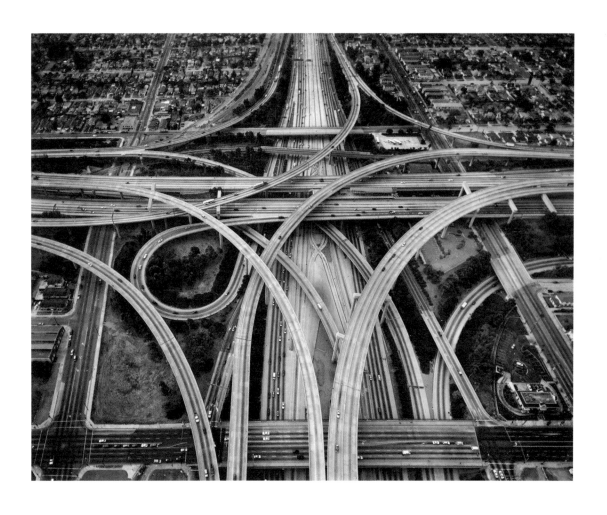

Edward Burtynsky, *Highway #1, Los Angeles, California, USA*, 2003

It is giant infrastructure projects that often find humans at their most impressive.

Judge Harry Pregerson Interchange

The Judge Harry Pregerson Directional Interchange in southern Los Angeles, California, is a four-level, 40-metre-high stack structure that connects US Route 105 with State Route 110. It was opened in 1993 and named after a popular and liberal judge of the US Court of Appeals for the Ninth Circuit, who halted several executions and reduced the lengths of sentences for minor offences.

It is one of the most awe-inspiring structures ever built, but it appears in no guidebooks, it is never spoken about as a work of culture and it remains utterly unobserved by most of the thousands of motorists who use it every day. It works so well that it is invisible – along with most of our public infrastructure. We know so much about our singers and actors, our novelists and television presenters, and next to nothing about our junctions and highways, aqueducts and sewage plants.

One result is that it's very easy to think of ourselves as an irredeemably wicked and mean-spirited animal, for we are at our worst in our love affairs, in our social media dramas, in our politics and our entertainments. And we are conversely at our best when we're linking up high-voltage power lines or carefully threading one highway into another.

The modern world seems perplexing and ugly in part because we stand too close to its wonders. We can be on a four-stack directional interchange turning a corner at 50 miles an hour and have no clue of the beauty we're partaking in. We're just in the car having an argument with our partner about the way they said 'always'. We're stuck within the circle of our ego. It doesn't help that nothing is ever explained to us properly. We can't understand most of the processes that create the structures around us. We don't know where things have come from, what most buildings are in the landscape or how most of our tools work. We may think this is a matter only for narrow-minded specialists or obsessives; in fact, it's material for anyone who wants to find reasons not to hate our species.

The point of a directional interchange is to keep cars moving at speed even while they complete what amounts to a 90° turn onto another highway, and it ingeniously overcomes the problem of 'weaving', where traffic exiting a road at one junction will interrupt traffic entering from another. Directional interchanges require two pairs of left-turning ramps that have to be raised above the two interchanging highways. To complete a left turn, drivers leave the highway via an exit on the right, go on a 270° loop on a clover-leaf-like ramp that crosses both highways, and then merge with traffic turning right from the opposite side of the interchange.

The world's first ever four-stack directional interchange, the Bill Keene Memorial Interchange, was built by the California Department of Transportation in 1949 where US Route 101 meets State Route 110. Eight more four-level stacks have since been added in the state and twenty-five others across America. They remain relatively rare anywhere else. There are three in the United Kingdom, one in Belgium, one in the Netherlands, one in Greece, one in South Africa and one in Australia.

None of this is too much about highways in the end. It's about what we should turn our minds to when we're very sad.

Julian Hinds Pumping Plant, Colorado
River Aqueduct, Hayfield Lake,
California, USA.

A place to contemplate our
ingenuity and care, and stave
off darkening skies.

Julian Hinds Pumping Plant

Driving along Interstate 10, in an empty region of the California desert, 55 miles east of Palm Springs, we can just make out a large rectangular building from which exit three large pipes that climb a third of the way up a barren mountainside before disappearing into the rocks. Nothing encourages us to take notice (there isn't even a sign on the road), and yet this peculiar bit of obscure and unheralded infrastructure is single-handedly responsible for ensuring that 23 million people across Southern California can have a bath, flush the toilet and water their Canyon Snow irises.

The building is a pumping plant built in 1941 under the supervision of one of the engineers of the Colorado River Aqueduct, Julian Hinds, and is the last of five stations that help propel water from the Colorado River up California's mountains from a reservoir, Lake Havasu, on the border with Arizona 126 miles away to the east. Inside the building, six gigantic 12,500-horsepower Westinghouse motors work twenty-four hours a day to drive water over 120 metres up the mountain, using electricity drawn from the Hoover Dam – at a cost, for this station alone, of some $10 million a year.

It is easy to feel extremely alone. Much about modern life separates us from our fellow humans. But this impression is invariably an illusion, for we remain tightly tied into a discreet web of dependence – simply one to which we struggle to give a name and a shape. Every time we turn on the tap, we are connected to the precise and thoughtful efforts of hundreds of people upstream from us: in Southern California, the controllers at Lake Havasu who monitor our water's levels and composition, and the engineers who look after the 242 miles that separate Havasu from Lake Mathews, the final reservoir on the outskirts of Los Angeles. The route includes 62 miles of canals, 92 miles of tunnels and 84 miles of buried conduits and siphons, through which 1,200,000 acre-feet of fresh water flow a year. Only a few days ago, the bathwater that we now lie in lapped the shoreline of a gigantic lake, across which windsurfers glided and through which catfish and bass swam. We may only have drawn a single glass – that sits on the table of the eerily quiet kitchen – but this modest draught travelled from Arizona in a collective body of water comprising millions and billions of litres, some of which will now be in a vase in the kitchen of a psychiatrist in Playa Vista and another bit of which will fill the yellow bucket of a 3-year-old child in a garden in Montecito Heights. We are not alone.

Buddhism recommends that we regularly strive to leave the prison of the self, with its unfortunate attachments and passions, in order to focus on phenomena outside of ourselves: the sound of birds, the rustle of leaves, the fall of raindrops. We might in homage focus our minds on the drip of the bathroom tap, for it too may provide a route out of the morose culs-de-sac of our nature and lift us into an unsuspected world of pipes and stations that are operated in a collaborative and meticulous spirit of what we may as well term love.

High Park Sewage Pumping Station,
195 Spring Road, Toronto, Canada.

Part of a world we depend on and are
never invited to see or understand.

High Park Sewage Pumping Station

Toronto is, perhaps, one of the world's less inspiring cities. The guidebooks try hard to get us to go to Ripley's Aquarium, or up the CN Tower; the Royal Ontario Museum has some interesting fossils and birds and some poignant canoes that the indigenous people used to ride in before their lands were seized and their children murdered by Europeans. And for those who enjoy that sort of thing, there's an extravagant Edwardian castle called Casa Loma on a hill or, when inspiration has properly waned, a Distillery Historic District filled with small boutiques selling craftwork and jewellery. Still, much of the time, we may simply want to remain in our hotel room.

This was not the way that tourism used to be done. Traditionally, on arrival in a new town or city, visitors would ask to be shown the fortifications, the stock exchange and the waterworks. They understood a place not through its junk-filled boutiques or galleries but – far more usefully – via its civic and military infrastructure.

The same principle should continue to apply today, for nowhere is boring for long once we ask where the poo flows or the power comes in. These matters belong to a hidden web of services that illuminate the spirit of a city and its people and evoke an unshowy reality that grounds and stabilises us.

The world is littered with obscure buildings, boxes, roadside sheds and unmarked huts that contribute to a feeling that we don't understand the wider framework of society and that we are the playthings of obscure forces. Small children are at least wise enough to ask: they insist on being told what's in the grey cabin at the end of the road or what lies beneath the large manhole cover. But most parents do such a good job of fending off their enquiries that by the time they are 8, they have stopped asking entirely and want to watch TV instead.

We should resume where we left off many years ago. On a visit to Toronto, we should dare to get properly to grips with the sewage system. If we are fortunate, we might end up going for a walk in High Park and there coming across a brown, one-storey brick box the size of a shipping container known (or rather not very well known) as the High Park Sewage Pumping station. Inside, a powerful motor is responsible for pushing tonnes of the area's poo from a concrete-lined chamber a kilometre or two east to the city's second largest wastewater facility near the mouth of the Humber River, the Humber Treatment Plant, a walled-off, awe-inspiring monolith unmentioned in any tourist publication, with a remarkable capacity to treat 473,000 cubic metres of waste per day.

Montaigne tells us that in ancient Egypt, it was the custom in the middle of feasts for servants to enter bearing skeletons, to remind the revellers of reality at a time when they might be most at risk of forgetting it. In a similar spirit, in the future, wiser cities wouldn't just bury their sewage plants and pumps behind some trees in a park. They would illuminate them, hand out maps of them to tourists and build a gigantic transparent piece of pipe in the middle of the city so that all citizens could watch their debris flow by every new day. Such vivid evidence of our common fleshly reality would help us lose our fear of not being good enough and weaken our sense of intimidation in front of so-called important people. Sewage systems shouldn't merely secretly spirit away our waste; they should – alongside galleries and temples – be given a chance to educate and cheer us.

Killala Bay Cable Landing Station,
County Mayo, Ireland.

It's not in their interests for us
to know about this, but it's very
much in ours.

Killala Bay Landing Station

Some of the reason why we are likely to have become sad and ill is that we have spent far too long at our screens. And the problem with these silicon-chip devices is that they are in the habit of making many things feel very easy, too easy, and of making other things feel hard, too hard.

The internet is founded on an aspiration to dissolve time and space. Everything should be immediate. No sooner have we formulated a question than we should have its answer; no sooner have we developed an appetite than we should satisfy it. Nothing should elude our will.

This is beguiling but also, over any length of time, poisonous, for most of what is valuable depends on a capacity to endure delay, frustration, ambiguity and boredom. If we rely on a tool that gives us everything we want, we will end up with nothing of what we need. While sparing us multiple efforts, our technology weakens our muscles for the labours that a good life demands. If we only have to click and drag, point and expand, if everything can be translated and solved by someone else, we will think it impossible that other bits of life should remain intimidatingly hard: that we may need to explain ourselves patiently to a partner; that we may have to seduce someone through empathetic understanding; that we might need to spend years patiently writing a book or labour at securing a degree or founding a business.

The internet's speed and simplicity don't prepare us for the ongoing trickiness of the rest of existence; they spoil us for the efforts we'll continue to have to make. Like an early inheritance for an indulged child, they drain us of the will to fight.

This is why it can be necessary and liberating to realise that the internet's apparent seamlessness is really an elaborate piece of trickery. It feels light, easy and free, but it is anything but. It was built by people in heavy boots with shovels and pickaxes; it was thought through by precise engineers. Every single full stop has had hours of coding behind it; nothing on a screen ever just landed there. The internet generates heat, it needs storage centres the size of airports, it pollutes rivers. We are messaging someone in Sao Paolo not by magic but because two vessels – the *Ile de Brehat* and *Ile de Sein* – spent two years laboriously laying down the EllaLink undersea cable between Portugal and Brazil. Our posts about our toddler are sitting in the Facebook data centre in Iowa, and our searches for a local Vietnamese restaurant are being routed through a Google facility in Oregon. The PDF we received from Sydney passed along the Southern Cross Cable Network, with shoals of fish swimming above it, via a plant in Hawaii. Our emojis aren't running on the holy spirit; they are burning coal.

The need for another kind of tourism opens up, one focused on the landscape of the internet that no one wants us to know about, on the mysterious fibres that run beneath our oceans and the warehouses lined with banks of computers. On such journeys, we might end up in the picturesque village of Killala in Ireland, where in a nondescript building the size of a petrol station, nearly the entire internet traffic between Western Europe and the Eastern Seaboard of America is routed. This is where your searches for lesbian threesomes, the emails to your mother, the stalking of your ex-partner and the anguished enquiries about symptoms for bowel cancer have passed.

We will be prisoners until we realise the extent to which the masters of the internet are mesmerising us. It's time to stop using our computers as divine toys; they are the work of some very clever and hard-headed people who are trying to anaesthetise us into passivity while themselves labouring extraordinarily hard in the background. We need to wake up and work out where the cables are buried.

Cities

Jessie Scott, *Weatherboard Bungalow
with Brick Cladding*, Coburg,
Victoria, Australia, 2013.

How free we would be if only we
could liberate ourselves from the
belief that there is a centre, that
life is elsewhere.

Coburg

Much of our professional anxiety can be traced back to a belief that we should never, ever end up living in a 'boring' suburb – one like Coburg in Australia, 9 kilometres north of Melbourne's central business district. To do so would mean abandoning any claim to being interesting, vibrant or alive; we'd be resigning ourselves to mediocrity and tedium. And therefore, in order to be able to afford to live closer to the centre, we have to work extremely hard; we are constantly scared that we might lose our jobs; we can rarely take a risk; we live in dread of every misstep.

Our age is dominated by a fear of missing out, powered by a conviction that – somewhere in privileged and secret locations – lives are unfolding that are uncommonly exciting, sexually fulfilled, interesting, beautiful and content, just as most lives everywhere else are fated to be humdrum, mediocre and banal.

Evidence of this worry is clearly visible in property prices. A house close to the centre may cost double or treble the amount of an equivalent one a few kilometres away: it's possible to put a rather precise number on the horror of not being where it's at.

To live contentedly in the suburbs requires us to adopt a distinct perspective which, if we were able to acquire it, would free us to enjoy a great many more options and to walk with far less fear through our workplace dilemmas.

A philosophy of the suburbs doesn't deny that there are, here and there, pockets of excellence: people with unusually kind hearts; groups of friends who are especially alive to, and entertaining about, the absurd sides of life; creatives who are especially talented or stylish. But what it denies is that such qualities can handily be tied to a single clan or location. It insists that goodness is an elusive trait that is promiscuously scattered through society and is not to be equated with any one simplistic marker (a given school, an age bracket, a skin type, a religion, a job or a postal code). One of the most fascinating people we could ever hope to meet might be a retired geography teacher working at the garden centre, who graduated from a provincial college no one has ever heard of. We might glimpse one of the most beautiful people in the world in the frozen-food section of the supermarket. The best novel of the century might, at this very moment, be being written in a boring-looking house between the recycling plant and the station. We have as much chance of connecting with true greatness, sincerity, depth and purity in a forgotten province as in any hallowed centre.

Were we able to take the thought to heart, we would be able to stop scouring the globe restlessly in search of a metropolitan paradise. We would know that life is never simply elsewhere, and that it might – when we look with sufficient imagination and courage – be going on in its own way right here, right now.

Mirko Rotondi, *Timeless Hotel, #18,*
Kuala Lumpur, Malaysia, 2012.

It might be very sane to feel out of
our minds in the megalopolis.

Kuala Lumpur

It is the middle of the night in one of the largest cities in Southeast Asia. Maybe we arrived here in the late afternoon from another continent, or perhaps this – a bedroom on the forty-third floor – is home. Either way, we are feeling lost. Sleep refuses to come. We open the curtains and see the city before us: 10 million people stretching out across kilometres from Petaling Jaya in the east to Pandan Indah in the west. The Exchange and the Petronas Towers light up the enveloping tropical night.

We feel restless, haunted and uneasy. Thoughts come at us from all directions: memories from our childhood, apprehensions about the future, snatched lyrics of pop songs and lines from films. Adverts blink at us outside, beseeching us to buy Sangkaya coconut ice cream and Subaru 4×4s. On the television, Shila Amzah is singing about forbidden love, there are reruns of old episodes of *Manjalara* and a camel race is coming in from Jeddah on Al Arabiya.

It's easy to think it may just be us, that the problem must be some fragility in our own minds, but it can be therapeutic to hold on to another idea: that our occasional moods of paranoia, terror and isolation have to do with the intense peculiarities of modern cities. Nothing in our evolutionary history has prepared us to dwell in such places. Our particular upbringings may have given us a few distinct struggles, but a large part of our distemper can be attributed to trying to make ourselves at home amidst millions of strangers competing for attention, fighting for love, desperate to avoid humiliation and ruthless in their pursuit of status. For the largest part of our collective history, we lived in small groups: our identity was assured, our roles were clear. No one asked us who we were or what we had recently achieved. There were no business cards or trade conferences. The mission was basic but always evident; the options were limited, but so were the risks of ignominy and exclusion.

We are so inured to modern cities that it can be hard to see just how much they ask of us and the toll they exact. They continuously excite in us fantasies of success, fame and lust and, at the same time, terrify us with threats of punishment and stigmatisation. They press us closely together and keep us meticulously apart. They leave us to stare out of high-rise windows at one another in the night, wondering what troubles or joys strangers may be going through, and sometimes longing to meet.

We easily fall into doubts as to our own significance and direction. Nothing we are and do can ever measure up to the brilliance of the famous ones. We are humiliated by the scale of the ambition and achievements glimpsed out of the window. Our nothingness is proved not, as in past ages, by the gods or by nature, but by our fellow human beings who put up the Kuala Lumpur Tower or run the Mid Valley Megamall.

The Greeks thought a civilised city should allow us to see the countryside from the central square, so that the human and the natural would always remain in harmonious co-existence. Here, we would need a helicopter to allow us to see to the end of the sprawl and the edges of the forest at Gunung Nuang. It might take days to cross the city on foot and, even then, we might never find a way out.

The therapeutic element is paradoxical; it isn't that there is a particular solution. But there may be some relief in a diagnosis. We don't need to shoulder all the blame. By coming to cities as extreme as Kuala Lumpur, we can more clearly understand dynamics that are just as present, though less in evidence, in more modest but equally challenging conurbations.

Whatever their freedoms and excitements, cities force our psyches to submit to degrees of pressure we were not designed for. We aren't randomly miserable or insane; we were just not built for these towers of dreams.

Grand Canal, Venice, Italy.

Proof of how much we long for
beauty, and of how mistaken we have
been in trying to locate it.

Venice

One of the most widely accepted ideas espoused by modern architects, designers and cultural critics is that no one can really say what beauty is; the answer is always subjective, it is always only ever in the eyes of the beholder. That is why our modern cities are in the habit of looking extremely strange. The new opera house may resemble an inverted washing up bowl or a squashed rabbit, but that's just you – and you might be old or a 'snob'. And while the new violet and lime-green towers on the horizon may seem obviously monstrous in your eyes, that's a subjective opinion which it would be deeply inappropriate to assume that anyone else shares.

And yet, despite this official line, it is more than clear that, in reality, there is extremely widespread agreement about what a beautiful city might be. Whatever the architects or cultural relativists might claim, it's self-evidently not Frankfurt or Milton Keynes, Detroit or Santiago, Chengdu or Lille. The beautiful cities are Amsterdam (19 million visitors a year), Paris (30 million), Barcelona (32 million) and Venice (36 million). People show us what they think is beautiful in a very simple and clear way: by going there. The best indicator of underlying agreement about urban design is tourist numbers.

People want to live in and visit places with regular street patterns, four- or five-storey buildings (at most), a tight core, symmetrical façades with variegated window sizes, mixed residential and commercial zones and a repeated vernacular style that fits in with the prevailing climate, geography and culture. It sounds relatively simple, and it is. We can look at places as distinct as Kyoto and San Francisco, York and Quito and swiftly perceive the broad principles of a good city.

The problem is that we have fetishised beauty as if it might be the result of divine inspiration or never-to-be-repeated genius. We have honoured successful cities by turning them into theme parks and setting them in aspic. We have not extrapolated outwards from their specific examples towards universally applicable rules of city-making that we might take back home and set to work on in our own locations. We are too tolerant of ugliness in certain places and too mystical about beauty in others.

Venice is, of course, astonishingly pretty, but we are killing it with our derivative and sterile admiration. A true homage would mean not trying to add yet more crowds to St Mark's Square; it would involve attempting to apply to other cities in the world some of the lessons that have made this particular settlement such a success. We wouldn't be building a pastiche (that would be a misunderstood lesson), but playing another, sympathetic tune on the keyboard of urbanism.

The promise of industrialisation has been to make what is good and desirable widely available. We have done this with great success around clothes and phones, cars and sofas; no longer are these accessible only to a narrow aristocratic clique. We should do the same with cities, travelling to the beautiful ones to learn their lessons and then applying these everywhere, so that fewer people might need to go to, and thereby help destroy, the legendary masterworks of the urban past.

Garry Winogrand, *Paris, France*,
c. 1969.

The street as the most interesting
film we could ever watch.

Paris

One of the finest therapeutic activities we can undertake in cities is also one of the simplest and the most readily available: going out for a walk. In mid-19th-century Paris, this activity was for the first time accorded a name. To wander the city was to be a *flâneur,* someone who ambled down boulevards and explored side streets, not to get anywhere in particular, but for the sheer pleasure of being able to see their fellow citizens, of all ages and classes, running errands, taking children to school, meeting business associates and – perhaps – conducting a love affair or plotting a murder. The *flâneurs* were protesting against the pressure to look vacantly down at their feet and pretend that they were all alone in the city: their curiosity was correcting the alienation of our hurried, solipsistic modern age. At the very dawn of the mass entertainment industry, the *flâneurs* were insisting that nothing could rival the novelistic pleasures of discreetly studying strangers in the street.

Paris lent itself particularly well to the wanderings of the *flâneurs.* Its broad boulevards, pavement cafés, covered arcades and compact parks immediately brought them into contact with a varied cast of characters around which speculations could take form. In the 1960s, the *flâneur* acquired a camera: what became known as 'street photography' added a recording mechanism to capture the contingent beauty and interest of the urban theatre. In 1969, Garry Winogrand, arguably the greatest street photographer the world has yet known, made a trip to Paris from his native New York. His image of a café in Montparnasse immediately invites us to imagine the stories that might be at play. The man in the polo neck, the pampered son of an industrialist doing a degree in hermeneutics at the Sorbonne, has just asked the woman in white, who was recently left by her Dutch boyfriend and had solemnly taken a decision not to trust men for a long while, if it would be OK for him to sit next to her. The woman on the right has pretended not to notice and doesn't often get approached by men (but might be off to meet her civil service lover, twice her age, in an apartment nearby). The waiter, an excitable man who could have been a boxer when younger, chiefly doesn't want trouble, unless we're looking for a table?

We don't need very much to start the game: a face is enough, and no more than a few seconds. Some of the pleasure comes from a recognition that we are not alone with our dilemmas and sufferings. Alone in our room, we may feel like the only ones in trouble; out on the street, we see that life spares nobody their share of anxiety and disarray. We are drawn out of ourselves; our problems diminish in scale, relativised by the old man crossing the street painfully slowly or the disabled woman patiently feeding a pigeon. There are multiple opportunities, too, to fall in love; not the sort of love that will result in marriage and children and long domestic evenings squabbling about where to spend the holidays, but the idyllic, weightless, boundless sort of love that comes powerfully to mind when we pass a beautiful, intelligent face at a junction and imagine being allowed up to their apartment and there coming to understand the origins of their sadness, stroking their arm gently as they describe the early death of their beloved father and their aspirations to paint abstract canvases or write a book of poems.

Edward Chao, *Illinois Center*
(Night), Chicago, Illinois, 2018.

The office as a source of rescue,
not just punishment.

Illinois Centre

It's common to think of the office as the place where we, sadly, cannot be ourselves. Here we have to wear formal clothes; we have to put things very carefully to others; we have to watch everything we say. Whereas home is, by delightful contrast, the place where we can let our true selves emerge. Here we can speak our minds; here we can lounge as we need to; here we can shout what we please.

It sounds – in theory – as if the advantage must lie solely at home. But we may reach a stage when, privately, we come to a rather different conclusion, and look forward to the office precisely because this place doesn't allow people to be 'themselves' without inhibition. We may acquire reverence for the rules of professional decorum that stop people uttering whatever they happen to be thinking, that inhibit us from sharing every whim and fancy, that force us to be circumspect, respectful and diffident. A place that allows people to be themselves can, in reality, turn into its own small version of hell.

As we cross the threshold of the gigantic corporation and put on our lanyard, we assume a professional manner which, while it isn't the deepest truth about us, is nevertheless a far more liveable version of who we are, both for others and for ourselves, than the untrammelled sincere one we are at home. Our office personas are tight-lipped about most of their agonies and longings; they don't let on about their envy and their lusts, their irritation and their sense of failure. They have no time for idle speculation on what might have been or regret over paths not chosen. They have no opportunity to worry about the long term or speculate on what strangers might be saying. They try to be helpful. They don't assume that other people will immediately know what they mean without having been told. They make an effort to teach. They'll induct novices carefully into their wishes.

They won't simply bang the table like a tinpot ruler and shout, 'Because I say so!' When they are feeling hard done by, they won't pick on the nearest person and throw their bad mood over them like slurry. They won't grunt. They'll try to make sense. They'll force themselves to be civilised. It may be fake – but that might, at points, be a very fine thing to be.

We're used to thinking of the office as the hard bit of life: here we come to work out how to ship lumber from Riga to Singapore, or to amortise loans from a pension scheme, or to settle rules on the use of acrylamide in potato crisp manufacture. It sounds complicated and it has its quirks, but over time, we're likely to realise that this is the simple part. What child's play financial engineering or company law are next to the infinitely more daunting tasks of trying to get someone to understand the way we need to be loved, or convincing a 14-year-old that we are, firmly, on their side. These are the truly nightmarish missions which we are never properly educated in. We may have done seven years of legal training, but at home we have never been offered even a single lesson in coping with the burdens of domestic existence. No one has any respect for the complexities of what they are trying to do; everyone assumes it should be easy and grows enraged and intolerant when it turns out it conclusively isn't.

No wonder we secretly long for the smell of cheap coffee, the bright overhead lighting and the efficient beginnings to yet another narrowly purposeful day. The office has its challenges, no doubt, but next to what might be waiting for us at home, this may be the holidays.

Oslo harbour with Oslo City Hall,
Norway, 1951.

Our true wish isn't to be known or
distinguished; it might just be to
belong to a dignified community.

Oslo Rådhus

The spirit of the times invests considerable energy in persuading us that what we really want is to make a lot of money, to be famous, to stand out from the crowd and to become 'someone'. But there are one or two rare places on earth that powerfully remind us that our true wishes lie elsewhere entirely: that what we desire, deep down, is a chance to belong to a community we can believe in.

The building of Oslo's city hall, the *rådhus*, began in 1930 to a design by the architects Arnstein Arneberg and Magnus Poulsson, and was finally completed, after suffering delays in World War II, in 1950. It is possibly the most elegant municipal centre ever put up, relying on pared-down modernist forms articulated in large medieval-style bricks allied inside with liberal amounts of wood panelling, brass and polished limestone. This is where the government of Oslo decides on its housing policies, where it allocates a budget for schools and kindergartens, where decisions are taken about the care of the elderly, where roads are mapped out and new kinds of traffic signs approved. Inside the main chamber, a tapestry by the artist Else Halling depicts the seven virtues of government in the hope of inspiring probity and wisdom in the assembled officials. On the west side of the building, there is a giant equestrian statue – by Anne Grimdalen – of the revered King Harald III of Norway (1015–1066), while a gigantic clock with a minimalist fascia on the east tower is visible across much of the capital.

It's what the building says, as much as what is done inside it, that counts. It whispers to all who pass it that belonging to this community can be a matter of immense and legitimate pride. However accomplished you might be, however rich and interesting your life, this can be secondary to your participation in the noble group life of the citizenry of Oslo.

The modern age typically leaves us entirely alone to make a mark solely through our own strengths. This may be a thrilling challenge for an energetic and uncommonly skilled minority, but for most of us, it is far too much. Oslo's city hall gives us a way out: we don't need to do it all by ourselves. Simply by virtue of participation in the collective, we can be enhanced and our position justified. We don't need to be unique; we can be just an ordinary citizen (perhaps we're employed to teach 5-year-olds how to sing, or we repair boilers in the hospital), but that – the rådhus is telling us – is very much good enough.

In many parts of the world, what belongs to everyone may be squalid and may have associations with all that is degraded and frightening. If we live in such places, we may want desperately to avoid 'public' housing, healthcare and education. And as a result, we may work exceptionally hard in order to afford a car in which no one else will ever ride, to outfit our home with a spotless kitchen that no one but us will ever use and to ensure that we can die in a hospital room uncontaminated by our typical fellow humans. Oslo, however, has another lesson for the planet. Along with a few other exceptional city governments (Zurich and Amsterdam come to mind), it lays on services that we would want to participate in whatever our levels of income – and it thereby drains us of our frenetic will to insulate ourselves from the mass and to achieve a position of distinction and walled-off privacy.

In a better world, the buildings that belonged to everyone would always exceed the palaces of the rich; it would be by throwing in our lot with the community that our own lives would be best justified and enhanced. We don't really want to be special at all. We want – far more importantly – to live in a community we can be proud of.

Jean-Jacques Lorin, *Restaurant, Omoide Yokocho, Shinjuku, Tokyo*, 2016.

For a modest sum, someone will enquire whether we're satisfied; someone will seem to care.

Omoide Yokocho

We know that what we should really have are friends, that what we really need is a project, that what we really crave is touch and that what would properly revive us is love. But those fine and beautiful things are not – in the actual conditions of life – always necessarily readily available. And that is why, in the fallen world we actually inhabit, it is a notable piece of good fortune that we can every now and then go and visit a place like Ayumu's restaurant in a tangle of streets just south of Shinjuku Station in Tokyo.

The restaurant has been there for ten years and we've known about it for three. It seats fifteen at the bar and a further twenty in small, quiet tables at the back. It's normally Yoshi or her daughter Fumiko who come and take our order. The menu changes regularly – Ayumu handwrites it himself – and specials of the day go on a board by the grill. There's no particular theme, it's whatever takes their fancy or happens to be in season. Yoshi is patient and, despite the bustle, makes us feel she has time; she understands that this might be a bit more difficult for us than for the others. The *tamagoyaki* is delicious; apparently this could be an evening to try out the sukiyaki. Or what about a heart-warming *nikujaga*, an idea which somehow makes Yoshi laugh a little and touch our arm in a maternal way (she can tell that we might be in need of beef, potatoes and some vegetables simmered for a few hours in a soy, sake and mirin sauce – a kindly dish for someone for whom not everything has gone right).

The restaurant is filled with small signs of care. The chopsticks are simple but weighty. The lighting lends itself to conspiracy. Someone went to a lot of trouble to source those padded chairs. Yoshi is back surprisingly fast. Just a few gyoza to keep us going. They're perfectly crisp yet yielding. It's been a while since anyone even appeared to care.

A beer or some water? Perhaps some cold sake? The questions are compact and clear. No one in this place asks anything that we can't answer; they don't cross-examine our thoughts and they never disagree with our choices. They don't ask us to take responsibility or lift our game, or suggest we take a long hard look at ourselves right now and stop pretending. They just wonder if we might fancy some edamame as well?

Money obviously cannot buy us what we truly want: the sincere regard of those we live among, a chance to contribute to the welfare of others, a sense that we are understood. But it can, at difficult points, at least buy us a few symbols of considerateness, and sometimes that might be the very best we can hope for, and that is realistically available to us, in our distinctly bathetic and radically imperfect lives. We do not always have the inner resources to find a meal the trivial thing it probably is.

A restaurant won't directly solve any of our deeper problems: it can't guide us through the maddening complexities of our domestic arrangements or help us build a satisfying career. What it can do is provide us with a much-needed degree of consolation. Here, we can be looked after for a couple of hours in a way we perhaps last knew as children when competent, kindly adults took it upon themselves to try to make us happy. Even as we battle through the trickier days of our lives, we're never too far from a quiet table and a menu – and Yoshi waiting with artfully feigned patience to take our order.

Underside of London Bridge, UK.

Looking south from the Thames
Embankment. The river speaks of
an alternative to the punishing
march of human time.

London Bridge

Above, hundreds of cars and buses pass by every hour. Phone calls are being made and plots are being hatched. Someone is organising an $11.7 million fundraising round for a biotech company ahead of a float in Hong Kong next March. At the nearby Old Bailey, a case is winding up involving a Canadian oil magnate and the brother-in-law of the president of Angola. Three people are – independently of one another – organising to go on dates at the restaurant on the top floor of the Tate Gallery. A mother employed in the commercial division of a city law firm is running across the bridge, thirty-five minutes late to pick up her 3-year-old from a nursery in Fulham.

The pressure on our lives is relentless and largely unavoidable. Yet there are opportunities for small moments of escape when we go and look at the river as it passes through the city. The buildings all around may house our practical needs and ambitions, but the flowing river cuts an alternative liquid channel through them that offers us a radically different perspective on our priorities and troubles.

The river remembers when the first exhausted, terrified groups of humans arrived at its banks, dressed in the hides of wolves, grunting obscurely. They worshipped the river as a divinity and made sacrifices to their gods in its shallows. Later, a primitive church was built nearby. A battle was fought. The Romans came and went. Corpses floated by. Severed heads bobbed up and down. Saxon children learned to swim from an embankment (now the site of the headquarters of an insurance company). One winter in the reign of Elizabeth I, the Thames froze over and the people held dances on the ice. A German bomber impaled itself nose first in the mud in the foggy autumn of 1943. The particularities of today – which loom so large in our own frantic minds – are immersed in a longer, grander story.

The river's oozing, viscous clay bed preserves memories. Down there is a phone someone threw away in a panic about their affair. A wedding ring was symbolically cast away one night in despair; a gun was abandoned in remorse. A child lost Nounou over the edge. So many have looked down forlornly and hoped for rescue. Our collected tears would form a stream of their own.

The water swirls around the piers, resists a moment, then is carried down towards the marshy flatlands of the estuary. It began to collect days ago in small streams up in the hills; it swelled in size and picked up speed, passing medieval churches, pubs, villas, car showrooms, a cricket pitch, a cemetery – and is now almost at its journey's end, heralded by the impatient squawk of seagulls and the occasional reckless grey seal venturing upstream in search of sand eels. No drop of water will be in the precise same place ever again, no waveform will ever be identical. The moments of our lives are equally unique, fugitive and unobserved.

In the middle of the status-conscious, materially minded city, there is an alternative voice, whispering consoling messages to us about the vanity of all things: this too shall pass. The river offers to return us to a position in which our worldly concerns are balanced by an equal attention to what is solitary, profound and sincere. We are fated to be hybrid beings, simultaneously material and soulful; we are creatures of the city and of the river. Bridges are where our two worlds interconnect. We should not merely cross them: we need also regularly to pause and hear what they are trying to tell us.

Laurent Hou, *Sindorim Station,
Seoul*, 2015.

A face seen for only a minute
holds the promise of all that
still eludes us.

Sindorim Station

We saw them for only a moment. They were heading southbound, on the line to Samseong. We'd transferred over on the Incheon line after meeting a friend in Guro, and for a moment, our eyes met on the escalator. It was a typical miniscule incident of connection, such as a large city (and especially its stations and trains) inspires every day.

Over time, our true relationship has become extremely difficult. It's now almost impossible to avoid areas of irritability. A simple word can set them – or us – off. Only yesterday there was another dispute about their cousin, and before that, about the bins. It's been so long since we were able to display the reserves of kindness and sweetness we still possess. We would like so much to be tender and innocent, as we were at the start; we aren't anything like the dour figures we appear to have become. We crave a chance to laugh and to adore.

We noticed them immediately on their way down. They were looking into the middle distance and had a trace of a smile, as if they had just thought of an incongruous incident or remark. Something about the way they held themselves implied an intelligent, slightly gauche manner, as though they were signalling how absurd they found the business of living, but that they were still committed to approaching its paradoxes with thoughtfulness and good humour.

We can imagine how we might be able to trust them with the odder sides of our personalities. Instead of withdrawing when we disclosed some of our ideas, they might come up with intriguing new suggestions of their own; they'd gladly join with us in a mutual conspiracy against the rest of the world. They would see us without the baggage of the past: there would be no legacy of hurts, no list of resentments and no grudges.

As we approach the ticket hall, we imagine how a life with them might develop. We'd laugh together over their old professor at Seoul National University. We'd be fascinated by each other's ideas about politics (they'd be interested in reforms to the constitution and might at one time have helped canvass votes for the Mirae Party). They might originally be from out of town, maybe Changwon or Cheongju. Perhaps their father was an engineer and their mother a dental hygienist. We'd discover unexpected, deep points of overlap in our interests and attitudes (the novels of Han Moo-sook or *pansori* music). Routine activities would become fun in their company; we'd tease each other while cleaning the bathroom. It would be adventure enough just to explore the supermarket aisles with them.

We won't, of course, ever know them – but the point isn't to arrive at an accurate vision of who this particular person really is. Something larger and more important is at stake in our fantasies in the station. A new idea is starting to develop: a better relationship could be possible; there might be someone (there might even be many) around whom life could be sweeter and more exciting. The disappointments of the present do not have to be a guide to the future. There continue to be grounds for hope. The city has plenty more stories to offer us.

Garry Winogrand, Central Park Zoo,
New York, c. 1963.

A place to contemplate who
really belongs behind glass.

Central Park Zoo

A person would have to be extremely hard-hearted to find it 'fun' to go to the zoo. Nevertheless, it's a hugely important activity: shocking, cathartic, necessary – like going to a funeral or to visit a friend in prison or a hospice. We aren't quite the same afterwards, and that's the point. We should definitely think twice before taking a child.

Seldom has the relationship between humans and animals felt more laden with tragic misunderstanding than in Garry Winogrand's 1963 picture of a beluga whale and its attendant window cleaner in Central Park Zoo in Manhattan. Extraordinarily, given where it's ended up – far from its natural habitat, in the vicinity of Macy's and MoMA – the beluga seems to bear no grudges; it sports the sort of smile that an upbeat 5-year-old would give it. If it could speak (in our language, for it does well enough in its own), it would chiefly express bemusement: *What have you humans dreamt up now?* It might sigh like a forgiving grandfather. This morning there were some little ones making faces, and earlier in the week there were some people with gigantic balls of candyfloss trying to offer it lunch (in fact, it eats mostly octopus and walleye pollock). And now this ... that stick-like thing might be some sort of weapon, but by this stage, it's clear to the whale that panic leads nowhere.

Part of the ridiculousness of the man (and by extension the self-important dragnet-making species to which he belongs) is how dolled up he is for his role. He's come with a special hat and quasi-military uniform to clean a window for the prison cell of an abducted Arctic cetacean held against its will in a corner of a New York park.

Nevertheless, the beluga maintains only good feelings towards its captor, perhaps because it knows – in its clever whale-mind – that he is some sort of captive too. This is no life for him either. It's late and he should be at home with his partner (its own is, after all, just next to it). Both are victims.

One impulse might be to try to set the whale free, but it would be tricky. The beluga would never fit in a cab. It would have expired – noisily so; they're known as the 'canaries of the ocean' – long before we ever reached the East River. For better and for worse, this is its permanent and last home.

In zoos, we look on at animals with bemusement, and they look back at us with pity. It's never clearer that there may be a mistake about who should be in a cage, enclosure or aquarium or about who deserves to be thought of as the 'animal', with all the pejorative associations of that word. The right tone to adopt in zoos is funereal seriousness. We aren't dreaming. There is something very wrong with our sort, and by looking deep into animals' eyes, we may start to pick up a few hints as to what that might be.

History

San Juan River, Utah, USA.

Some 300 million years of time made
visible and, importantly, memorable.

San Juan River

One of our greatest difficulties – which gives us problems in so many areas – is that we can't understand time. However often the facts are explained to us, they keep slipping from our minds. Our myopia is partly rooted in our lifespan: the eighty or so years we have on the planet tend to power a steadfast background sense of what a 'long time' might mean. Our brains dwell predominantly in the here and now, for there seems no efficiency or reward in having too many thoughts about what used to be or what is to come. Three months from now already feels very remote; a decade before our birth has a primaeval sheen to it; five years away is unimaginable.

These biases are understandable, but they make things far harder than necessary. We continuously exaggerate both the importance of setbacks in our individual lives and, more broadly, the significance of these lives within the greater span of planetary existence. As a result, we panic far more than we should and we laugh far less than we might. An animal that thinks of a five-hour journey as 'long' or a three-minute download time as 'slow' is going to have problems finding perspective around a great many of its travails.

The sharp bends in the San Juan River in southeastern Utah appear to know our problem well enough and offer us a powerful solution to it. We cannot spend more than a moment in their company without sensing that we are being told something very powerful about time; more specifically, how much of it there has been – and how little of that has been about us, the current president, the shocking headlines and the mesmerising scandal. The San Juan River has very slowly cut a winding 300-metre-deep canyon through 300 million years of time. The rocks at the river bottom date back to the Palaeozoic period, some 70 million years before the dinosaurs. The Earth's continents were at that point fused together into the giant landmass of Pangaea, the apex predator was the *Dimetrodon*, the land was populated by synapsids and diapsids and the seas were filled with molluscs, echinoderms and brachiopods. The air buzzed with dragonflies the size of eagles.

We forget most of what we've ever been taught about time, but it pays to keep a few basic facts in mind:

- Age of the Earth: 4.543 billion years
- First life on Earth: 3.77 billion years ago
- First land animal: 428 million years ago
- First dinosaurs: 243 million years ago
- First *Homo sapiens*: 200,000 years ago
- Birth of agriculture: 10,000 years ago
- Early dynastic period in Egypt: 5,000 years ago
- Height of the Roman Empire: 1,920 years ago
- First photograph: 195 years ago (at the time of writing)
- First powered flight: 118 years ago
- Last moment of despair: 5 days ago

Even as we scan the list, our attention may blur: a few million here or billion there are hard concepts to fix in the understanding. The San Juan River appreciates the difficulty and won't set us any tests. It is content, through its majestic beauty, to make an overall point that should reach us through our senses as much as it does through our understanding. It really only wants to say one very simple thing to us nonexperts in its ancient gravelly voice: that it is very, very old, and that we are very, very short-lived. And on that basis alone, we should probably surrender our absurd and painful sense of the seriousness and importance of all that we are and do.

Arco di Riccardo, Trieste, Italy,
built 1st century CE.

Bits of the past linger inside us,
and the present moulds itself
around them.

Arco di Riccardo

The arch – referred to locally as the Arch of Richard for reasons no one can now entirely remember – was put up by the Romans in their city of Tergeste, now modern Trieste, in around 33 BCE when the future Emperor Augustus was coming to power.

It formed part of an extensive programme of works for the city, which included new city walls, baths and a library. The architect would have been well known; newcomers would have been awed. Yet as the centuries passed, the Romans lost their empire. The statues that had once adorned the arch were pillaged and the city was annexed by one warlord after another. The surrounding area decayed and anyone who could moved away. People chiselled out lumps of stone from the arch to repair their own homes; in winter, ice expanded in the cracks, gradually weakening the entire fabric.

A tenement building was erected beside the arch, casually making use of one of its piers as part of the side wall and destroying its once noble symmetry. Today, the arch juts straight out of a restaurant, famed in the area for its orecchiette with fresh tuna and swordfish with aubergine purée.

For those who knew the arch when it was built, it might be confounding to see it battered, mutilated and half buried. But we can take pride in its survival as well. The past may be substantially submerged, but bits of it live on; things don't disappear entirely. We can make our peace with what remains and integrate its irregular masonry into our present. We can live promiscuously among the debris of different ages. An old triumphal arch adorned with statues might magnanimously offer to hold up a beam of a family restaurant where, after much thought, we may order the *maccheroncini* with red shrimp.

Surprising us in the middle of a street with its ancientness, the arch offers to release us from the intimidating aspects of our own times. Everything that seems impressive or important today will gradually lose its prestige. Our urgent debates will be known only to a few scholars, who will struggle to find an audience; our current celebrities will seem like the most old-fashioned people in the world and then will be forgotten entirely; our most radical ideas will sound incomprehensible; everything that motivates or disturbs us will be forgotten. Our personal errors will count for nothing in the sweep of history, and no one will remember or care about our failings. The things that loom so large, and are so painful and agitating, in our own picture of our lives will leave almost no trace.

To the Romans who built the arch, it would have seemed that the fall of their empire was the fall of the entire world. They could not begin to imagine that the planet would ultimately survive well enough without them, and that new – and in significant ways much better – forms of society would eventually emerge.

At some point in the future, someone will look on a decayed fragment of New York, Tokyo or London and wonder, for a moment, about what we, who lived then, were like – and all their ideas will be wrong and we will be free.

The Alcobaça Monastery, Alcobaça,
Portugal, founded in the 12th
century CE.

An important part of us may be
lodged in cultures and times very
distant from our own.

Alcobaça Monastery

An hour's drive north of Lisbon, in the hills a few kilometres from the coast, lies the picturesque town of Alcobaça, famous for hosting what is perhaps Portugal's most beautiful work of architecture: the Alcobaça Monastery, founded in 1178 by King Afonso I and constructed over the next two centuries in the austere, undecorated style of the Cistercians. It's been a museum since Portugal banned religious orders in 1834, but still powerfully conveys its original atmosphere. We can look around the monks' bedrooms, their tiled dining room, their enormous pared-down church (more like a cathedral) and their solemn cloister, the Cloister of Silence, with its columns carved in the shapes of fantastical animals and its views out onto an immaculate garden and a trickling Renaissance water basin.

By the end of the visit, we might register an unfamiliar and somewhat peculiar feeling for which nothing has directly prepared us and which it might be hard to interpret or share successfully with our travelling companions (intent on making it to nearby Nazaré for lunch): the building is calling to us. Quite what it's saying is indistinct, but it's something about changing our career, the importance of silence and reflection, living more closely with people who share our values and dedicating ourselves to a greater degree of thoughtfulness. And conversely, it seems to be rebuking us (in the most polite way) for other things: for our hunger for approval, for squandering our energies, for the frivolity and superficiality of our social lives.

It isn't that we would literally want to become a monk; we hate rules, we don't believe and we love to lie in. But that's not how encounters with the past should work; we shouldn't need to want the totality of an era or a creed to be able to draw important benefit from it.

When it comes to knowing how to approach history, we're often presented with two awkward options. The first, naïve one, that owes much to a child's imagination, is that we try to lose ourselves in another age entirely: that we picture ourselves as a monk writing out passages of the Bible on vellum, or a Viking leading a brave band of soldiers, or a princess preparing for marriage in a castle in ancient Japan. The other, apparently more sensible approach, is to put aside all our own concerns and dedicate ourselves to the facts and the data without the intrusion of our personalities: history for history's sake.

The point is neither to go down the path of escapism nor to commit ourselves to rigorous scholarship. We should use history for inspiration; to lend encouragement to sides of our nature and to ideas which our own times have unfairly neglected.

However comfortable we are with the present, there will be parts of us that more fairly belong elsewhere – in 11th-century West Africa or 17th-century India, in the writings of a medieval Alexandrian poet or the song cycle of a German Romantic composer – in ways that we should strive to understand and accommodate. Some of the mission of our travels should be to bolster the unsupported parts of ourselves by bringing them into contact with more developed instances of our own latent tendencies.

In the car on the way to lunch in Nazaré, we might – still under the influence of the monastery – think of a range of modest but important ways in which our lives could be altered in the direction of greater focus, sincerity and reflection. We aren't going to join a religious order, but we might vow to switch off our phones completely for twenty-four hours once a week, look for a more tight-knit and honest group of friends or think of how we might live with far fewer belongings somewhere that could be at once basic and yet dignified. Without anyone noticing, we'll have started to do true justice to history – by learning to borrow from it.

Océlotl Cuauhxicalli, a jaguar-
shaped stone vessel to hold the
hearts of sacrificial victims,
Aztec, c. 1250–1500 CE. National
Museum of Anthropology, Mexico City,
Mexico.

The past as a guide to the submerged
follies of the present.

Tenochtitlan

The customary attitude of anyone approaching an ancient culture in the modern age is immense respect. We're looking to be impressed, to learn and to put our prejudices and assumptions aside. This is the mentality with which we are likely to start a tour of the National Museum of Anthropology in Mexico City, one-time Tenochtitlan, the capital of the Aztec peoples. Soon after we begin, we will be confronted by a large jaguar-shaped stone vessel – elegantly carved – which, a caption will inform us, used to hold the hearts of victims who were being sacrificed to the sun god Huitzilopochtli a few metres from where we're now standing.

The Aztecs proposed that there had once been many gods in the world and that they had squabbled in a way that made things difficult for humanity. The young god Huitzilopochtli defeated his treacherous siblings and became the furious, but life-giving, sun, separating day from night and making crops grow. The problem was that he needed to be kept going by a constant supply of human hearts, or else his rays would fade and everyone would die. So pyramids were built in all Aztec cities, at the top of which priests would – every day – cut open the torsos of a dozen or so victims with a flint knife and take their hearts out and hold them up beseechingly to Huitzilopochtli. The bodies were thrown down the steps to be eaten by animals.

Unfortunately, Huitzilopochtli wasn't the only god who needed to be encouraged. There was also one called Tlaloc (a caption by a small bath-like container informs us). He was the god of rain, water and fertility, and he needed human sacrifices too, though in his case, he required something very special: the tears of children under 10, as well as their hearts. So priests would have to buy children off poorer parents (who couldn't say no), make them cry (this bit wouldn't have been hard), collect their tears in a bath and then kill them too – or else the rains would fail and all the crops would die.

This is no one-off. Every society that has ever lived has practised rituals and held beliefs that – when we look at them dispassionately – emerge as either repulsive or insane or both. Crucially, *there is no reason why our own age should be any exception.* It may be easier to see the lunacies of other times, and we can tell rather quickly what is eccentric in a foreign culture, but that doesn't mean that our own societies are spared their fair share of absurdities.

The Aztecs certainly never thought that they held any sort of curious ideas (they were just doing what they needed to do to keep the sun and the rain in order) and nor, for that matter, did the Thracians, the Carthaginians, the Mongols or the Americans of the 1950s.

This should give us hope. Many of us feel, in the privacy of our minds, that some of the most sacred and popular beliefs of our own times (about what is right and wrong, about who should be revered and what cannot be mentioned) make no sense at all. But we don't dare to say so – or we would be (metaphorically) killed, just like an impudent inhabitant of Tenochtitlan who had cast doubt on the cult of Huitzilopochtli. Yet the fear doesn't mean we shouldn't continue with our scepticism. A journey into the past can strengthen us, through a reminder that we are almost guaranteed to be living among ideas which will rightly mortify later ages. It might take 400 years, but the strangeness will eventually become self-evident.

In the meantime, we may have to keep very quiet, but we don't have to stop doubting.

Walker Evans, *City Lunch Counter,
New York*, 1929.

We should learn to look at the
present with an awareness of
its eventual transformation into
'history'.

Corner of Lexington Avenue and 44th Street

It can be especially hard to imagine that all that now exists will one day belong to 'history'. The opinions we espouse, the clothes we wear, the buildings we put up and the sort of relationships we have, all these will eventually be deemed to have belonged to a distinct historical period, whose identity currently eludes easy recognition or summary. The present moment just feels fluid and boundless, incapable of being compressed into anything as restricted as an 'era'. We glance down at other periods of history from our vantage point in the present but can't imagine ourselves being wrapped up into anything as narrow as an 'age' in turn.

Our myopia has its costs. We miss being on the lookout for the particularities of our time. We don't notice how precious everything is – and how fragile and strange.

In early 1929, the photographer Walker Evans went around Manhattan shooting ordinary people having ordinary lunches in ordinary places. At the corner of Lexington Avenue and 44th Street, he came across a man (on the left in the picture) who thought he was just leaning forward to have another sip of milk, that drink of innocence, but who ended up entering history, just as surely as Napoleon or the Ming Emperor Zhu Changluo. We feel pained for the man at having to carry off this difficult double act; he didn't even have a chance to finish his sandwich and he might have chosen another, less festive kind of headwear if he had known that he was being signed up for eternity. The figure next to him is comparably unprepared and oblivious, though he seems to have walked into history from another, earlier era, perhaps the 1890s or before the Flood. Even his food is distinctly historic, as if he'd eschewed modern fare in favour of something more antediluvian like a kipper or a rabbit. As for the man on the right, he's doing his best to stay out of it. He has aspirations to appear 'normal' and 'universal' and steadily avoids our gaze while (maybe) doing a quiet burp. But he can't escape time either. With his combed-back hair and steely, inscrutable eyes, we recognise him as a cousin of Charles de Gaulle or a nephew of Harold Macmillan. He, too, won't be able to dawdle in the shapeless present forever; he, too, will have to join history.

None of Walker Evans' characters could have known that they would eventually form a small part of a gigantic enterprise called 'the early 20th century', which would have its own colours, lights, associations and hats.

Knowing what will inevitably happen, we might at points go out and look around at the present day as if it were already on the way to being the past it will eventually be categorised as. We might choose any place, as humdrum and as accessible as possible – the phone repair shop, the park, a restaurant, our kitchen – and, without any need for a camera, attempt to perceive what might touch, delight and move our successors in a future that is slowly gathering pace offstage. We might, alongside our journeys through space, learn to become melancholy travellers through time.

Gardens

Vincent Van Gogh, *Tree trunks in the grass, late April 1890*, 1890.

We all have permission – and perhaps on occasion an active need – to lose our minds.

The Garden, Saint-Paul Asylum, Saint-Rémy-de-Provence

For many of us, a fundamental priority is that we should never, ever end up in an asylum, or as some might put it pejoratively, a madhouse, a loony bin or a place for crazies. We are – for understandable reasons – deeply wedded to the idea of our sanity.

And yet looked at more generously, 'sanity' is not an unassailable island with rigid or impregnable boundaries: it is a continent that is constantly suffused with waves of trouble, pain and confusion. A degree of mental perturbance belongs to health. A share of madness is, and should be, present in every good and sane life.

Vincent Van Gogh entered the Saint-Paul Asylum in Provence in May 1889 and was to remain there until May the following year. He had grown increasingly exhausted in the previous months, his mood veering between exultation and despair, visionary fervour and dejected self-loathing. At first, he spent a lot of time in bed – sleeping, thinking and writing to his brother. Then gradually he felt well enough to paint and did so both in his room and in the grounds. He particularly loved the asylum's gardens: its pine trees, caterpillars, butterflies and flowers (bluebells, dandelions and – most famously – irises). It was here that he painted some of his best-loved works; the Van Gogh we know was reborn in this walled garden in Provence.

Nature wasn't just a pretty spectacle, it was evidence of the human capacity to endure and overcome appalling degrees of loss and shame. This was a man who had thought very seriously of killing himself only months before; in nature, he found a stream of counter-arguments. His tree trunks were weathered and experienced, they had known storms and years of buffeting and damage by the wind, but they were hardy and determined. Growing around them, his dandelions appeared innocent, copious and hopeful.

Part of the reason we break is that we do not – ordinarily – allow ourselves to bend. We believe we have no option but to keep going, to put up a front and to be so-called brave. But recovery only begins the moment we accept that we cannot cope, that it has become too much and that the disturbances we have been warding off for too long have now got the better of us.

However alarming our state might be to those around us, we might almost be grateful for our collapse. A breakdown can be a prelude to a breakthrough. In the midst of our despair or mania, things may be rearranging themselves inside. We are, confusedly, expressing a longing for a new kind of life: a more caring relationship, a more authentic career path, a more compassionate acceptance of ourselves and our past.

One day, we might find ourselves in an asylum. We shouldn't despair that this is where we have ended up. Many have been here before us – and some of them understood life better than anyone. We should feel proud of how courageous we have been in admitting that we are defeated. At last we have an opportunity to cry, to think and to heal. We don't need to do very much; we can lie in bed for hours and when we feel up to it, at our own pace, go out for a quiet wander among the pine trees. The old way wasn't working; this is a new start.

When the sun comes out, we might find a comfortable bench from which to contemplate a medley of flowers with the sort of mystical delight, open-hearted joy and love for life known only to those who have, in their darkest moments, been tempted to give up entirely.

Patio de la Acequia, Palacio de
Generalife, Alhambra Palace,
Granada, Spain, originally
constructed 1238-1358.

We must cultivate our gardens,
for the whole earth can never be
made pure.

Patio de la Acequia, Granada

The idea of a garden has always been central to Islam for reasons that are at once hopeful, because nature is so beautiful, and deeply melancholy, because life itself can never be made perfect.

For Islam, the world we inhabit will always be mired in *khatīa* or sin. No human enterprise or institution can ever be without significant degrees of *dhanb* or wrongdoing: jealousy, stubbornness, rage and lack of forgiveness predominate. Only in the next life can we hope to escape the irritation and the agony; only in *jannah*, or paradise, will we be assured of true contentment. In paradise, according to the Qur'an, there will be flowing rivers, flowers, incorruptible waters and unchangeable milk, golden goblets, 'virgin companions of equal age' and rows of cushions set out in the balmy shade of fruit trees.

Yet because this might all be a long way off, Islam recommends an unusual technique to prevent us from losing our poise and despairing: we should become *bustani*, or gardeners. The enlightened should redirect their frustrations with the state of humanity towards the construction of a *hadiqa*, or walled garden. Within its limited circumference, with due modesty, it can be endowed with many of the qualities of the eventual garden of paradise. Our garden should have flowing water, some reflecting pools, symmetrical flower beds, fruit trees and places to sit. Everywhere that Muslim civilisation spread, gardens developed along with it, and in the drier regions, where nothing would grow, flowers and trees were represented on carpets, which functioned as miniature mobile gardens that could be carried on the back of a camel. When the Muslims reached southern Spain, the climate allowed them to create pieces of horticulture which astonish and seduce us to this day.

A telling observation about gardening is that almost everyone over the age of 65 is concerned with it, and almost no one in their late teens has ever evinced the slightest interest in it. The difference isn't coincidental. A person's enthusiasm for gardening is inversely correlated to their degree of hope for life in general. The more we believe that the whole of existence can be rendered perfect, that love and marriage can be idyllic, that our careers can reward us materially and honour us creatively, the less time we will have for beds of laurel or thyme, lavender or rosemary. Why would we let such minor interventions detain us when far greater perfection is within reach? But a few decades on, most of our dreams are liable to have taken a substantial hit, much of what we put our faith in professionally and romantically will have failed, and at that point we might be ready to look with different, and significantly more sympathetic, eyes at the consolations offered by cypress trees and myrtle hedges, geraniums and lilies of the valley. No longer will gardening be a petty distraction from a mighty destiny, but rather a shelter from gusts and squalls of despair.

Islam is appropriately wise in its ambitions. It doesn't tell its followers to plough themselves a farm, nor does it advise them to focus on a window box. The scale is carefully calibrated: neither too big to mire us in unmanageable expense and bureaucracy, nor too small to humiliate and sadden us. The garden becomes a perfect home for our remaining pleasures in a troubled world; it's where we can repair to contemplate islands of beauty once we have come to know and sorrowfully navigated oceans of pain.

Space

Harald Sohlberg, *Spring Evening,
Akershus*, 1913.

A time of day that acknowledges our
frailty and ushers in relief.

Dusk, Akershus Fortress, Oslo

Our thoughts are – nominally – free to go in any direction at any time of day or night. In practice, perhaps far more than we dare to admit, they remain tightly tied to wherever we happen to be on the Earth's twenty-four-hour axial journey around the Sun. There are ideas which make most sense to us at daybreak, others which have to wait for high noon and others that require the night to convince us.

There can be no more resonant span in this rotation than the interval we know as dusk, when the sun slips below the horizon and throws its beams across the lower atmosphere, rendering the sky – for up to forty minutes in the northern latitudes, and as little as twenty minutes in the equatorial ones – neither quite light nor quite dark.

Dusk fascinated the Norwegian artist Harald Sohlberg, who painted it dozens of times in locations around his native Oslo – not only because he found it 'beautiful', but in order to focus our attention on the transformations this time of day can perform for us psychologically. There might be many sorts of dusks around the world, but what they whisper to us tends to be very similar.

Throughout daylight hours, we are invited to be purposeful. Our horizons are limited to the human world. The shadows are short and our perspectives can grow so too. We push our miniscule part of history forward a few more millimetres: we send emails, call for meetings, attend a conference, write a paper. With the sun high in our meridian, we grow tall in our own estimations. We make plans, we accuse someone of disrespecting us, we get frustrated with our progress.

But then comes dusk with its range of contrary messages. A narrow band of cloud many miles away turns a brilliant crimson. Distances we had forgotten about make themselves felt. We are no longer the measure of all things. Whatever has agitated us recedes in importance. The moment bids us to loosen our mind's fervent hold on the memory of the missing document or the course of the tetchy meeting; for the first time in many hours, we know viscerally that these things, too, will pass.

Dusk invites all of us – the desperate, the anxious and the arrogant – into the shelter of night, where grown-up priorities can weigh less heavily on us. There is nothing more we can do to alter anything now; we will have to wait and keep faith. We must stop grandstanding. And for a few especially pained ones among us, dusk is there to confirm that it might all be OK, despite the hatred, the shame and the ignominy.

The miraculous thing about every day – often missed by people who are extremely busy, content or conceited – is that it will inevitably end. However dreadful it has been, and some days are mightily so, it will reach a close. And all the things that draw their seriousness from the height of the sun will be dimmed by the approach of night.

How unbalanced we would be if – by some technological innovation – we managed to banish night altogether. Dusk saves us through erasure. Without dusk, there would be no more recalibration and no time for our arrogance to abate nor for our anxiety to be absorbed. We can be grateful that, despite all our gadgets and our pride, the wisdom of dusk is only ever a few hours away.

Alberto Ghizzi Panizza, European
Southern Observatory's (ESO)
Very Large Telescope (VLT) in
Atacama Desert, Paranal, Chile.

The sight of the universe returns us
to manageable proportions.

Paranal Observatory, Chile

The four 8.2-metre-diameter telescopes that sit on top of Mount Paranal in Chile's Atacama Desert were constructed (by a coalition of European countries) ostensibly in order to study the universe, in particular to explore gamma-ray bursts, detect gravitational wave forces and search for exoplanets. More accurately, however, these masterpieces of science have excelled at quelling our spirits and reconciling us to our fate by artfully reminding us of our beautifully negligible place in the totality of cosmic space and time.

In the rainshadow of the Andes, it is clear almost every night in this part of Chile, and as soon as twilight ends, the most sublime and redemptively terrifying display begins. The atmosphere seems to peel away and we are left standing on a small promontory on the edge of galactic infinity. There are more than 100 billion stars above us. Light takes 100,000 years to pass from one extremity of the Milky Way to the other. At the centre is a black hole, millions of times more massive than our Sun, around which we are spiralling once every 240 million years. Our galaxy is one of many huddling together in what is sweetly called the Local Cluster: itself a tiny, forgettable, random province in the vastly grander scheme of the comprehensible cosmos.

The brightest star in the Chilean night sky is Sirius, 8.6 light years away. The nearest – Proxima Centauri – is still an utterly unreachable 4.2 light years away. With the naked eye, we can see Omega Centauri, a 12-billion-year-old globular cluster packed with 10 million stars. Through a modest pair of binoculars, we may study the Centaurus A galaxy (NGC 5128), the fifth brightest in the sky, 12 million light years away and containing at its centre a super-massive black hole of 55 million solar masses, ejecting X-ray jets thousands of light years long.

All this is not a fantasy or a dream or a mystic vision. It's a sober, accurate, slowly assembled description of reality. We can make no personal sense of why the cosmos exists; it is governed by rules of almost unimaginable complexity and abstraction that make no reference to anything we can touch or feel. There is no human reason why we are here, no goal we are supposed to reach, no task we are required to fulfil. From the point of view of the galaxy and of the whole universe, our hopes and regrets are of no importance, our blunders can do no harm, our errors will have no impact. Our actions count for zero; it doesn't matter what we do.

As we contemplate the Milky Way from our Chilean vantage point, we shrink down to size. By recalling that we, and our world, are of no ultimate significance, we're not really saying that we should stop caring. Rather, we're reducing our responsibility to bearable proportions. We're not preaching complacency to ourselves; we're keeping our panic and gloom at bay so that we can turn our more settled minds to a proper analysis of what we are capable of. There are people who don't care enough, and they may need a very different intervention, but we may be among those caught up in a poignantly odd situation. We may regularly need to care less for a time, in order best to serve those we love.

Adam Gold, *The View from the Window,*
London, 2016.

The spectacle is above us
everywhere.

The Kitchen Window Observatory, London

Fortunately, we don't need to go to one of the world's finest observatories – in the Atacama Desert in Chile, Mauna Kea in Hawaii or Mount Teide in Tenerife – to benefit from the wisdom of their powerful lenses. All we need is a well-positioned window ledge and a little patience.

In the autumn of 2016, the English photographer Adam Gold had recently returned from a lengthy stay in a hospital near London. He had been treated for depression that had lasted more than a year. Without wholly understanding the draw, he began to spend long evenings at the kitchen window of his small flat, from which he could – on a clear night, despite the lights of hundreds of houses nearby – gain an unexpectedly detailed view of the universe above. He could glimpse the planet Venus and there were sightings of the constell-ations of Boötes, Corona Borealis and Hercules. One night even offered up the Eta Aquariids meteor shower.

Sensing the healing effect of this night-time observation, Gold began to take a series of photographs dedicated to tracking events in the sky as he could spot them from his own window. He could, of course, have gained more astonishing vistas by going to a desert peak, but his point was precisely to remind us, and himself, of how much of the universe might continue to be observable even in a highly crowded, often frenetic and light-polluted metropolis. Many of his images deliberately retain, at their edges, reminders of their humdrum locations: the windowsill, a neighbour's window, a passing plane. We have no excuse for not accessing the cosmic perspective, wherever we might be; a measure of calm is always to hand.

The night sky doesn't address us in words. It doesn't argue with us. It appreciates that at times we need to see, rather than be told. The soothing message of the night is encoded in sensory elements. It bypasses our logical minds and stimulates hope in the emotional parts of our being. Like the smell of newly cut grass or the earth after rain, it affects us by bypassing our understanding.

The night reorients us. If we sleep, our dreams will be usefully unsettling and strange. The certainties of the daytime world will be upset. We'll learn that we still miss someone we were supposed to have forgotten a long time ago. Or that we're attracted to an enemy, or that we are more vulnerable than we had supposed. And if we can't sleep, under the light of the stars, we'll be able to come at our dilemmas from new and unfamiliar angles. The difference between hope and despair is often just a different way of telling stories from the same set of facts.

The 17th-century Dutch philosopher Spinoza made a famous distinction between two ways of contemplating existence. We could either see it egoistically, from our limited point of view, or as he put it, *sub specie durationis* (under the aspect of time). Or we could look at things universally and eternally: *sub specie aeternitatis* (under the aspect of eternity). For Spinoza, our nature means that we are divided between the two. Our fears and desires can pull us towards a time-bound, partial view. Yet our reasoned intelligence can equally well at privileged moments allow us – and here Spinoza becomes unexpectedly lyrical – to participate in eternal totality.

We don't need to wait until we have built our own observatory to participate in eternal totality. Tonight, our own window ledge will be more than enough.

Richard Misrach, *Untitled*, 2004.

Another world – as rich in
extraordinariness as the stars –
is waiting for us a few millimetres
below the water's surface.

Fernando de Noronha, Brazil

Compared with all the talk that surrounds the microscope and the telescope, the aeroplane and the rocket, strangely little is ever said about two equally innovative instruments that have opened up alternative worlds to us: the mask and the snorkel. Associated in our imaginations with summer holidays, their grander therapeutic missions have been obscured. Schoolchildren know all about the Wright brothers and the Apollo programme; but no one seems to have properly registered the birth of the diving mask (1933) and the J-shaped snorkel (1950). Seventy per cent of the planet may be ocean; less than one per cent of all photography and art concerns itself with what lies under the water. We have paid extravagant attention to the remote possibility of extraterrestrials and ignored the mesmerising reality of the whitemargin stargazer and the tassled scorpionfish.

More than 550 kilometres off the northern coast of Brazil, the beaches on the archipelago of Fernando de Noronha are one of the finer locations from which to launch ourselves into aquatic space. Dipping our heads under the water, we're offered one of the strangest split-screen sights in the world: through the upper half of the mask, we see the sun, the sky, a few palm trees and familiar wisps of cloud; through the lower half, beneath a faint line of what looks like mercury, all traces of familiarity are gone. There are no more hotel buffets and cocktails, roads or buildings, only sea sponges and coral, beds of variegated gravel and forests of dense seaweed interspersed with algae-coated rocks.

There are also some extremely odd-looking inhabitants. A vast, blue fish with a protruding jaw and a thoughtful expression looks over at us, as though it were coming to an important conclusion on a substantial subject. A beige crab makes its way across the seabed uncomplainingly, lugging along one massively enlarged yellow claw with which it might hope to fix itself lunch. There are schools of trunkfish; a stingray performs a landing manoeuvre in the sand; a rock lobster naps between two rocks that perfectly match its shell. Language struggles to get itself around the oddities that dwell here: the short-nosed batfish, the squirrel fish, the rock beauty. God may happily have given names to all the land animals but – understandably – may have lost momentum when it came to those beneath the waves.

It feels as if we had stepped into a very strange party whose members, perhaps after ingesting an unknown psychedelic, were pursuing their own dreams and projects without possibility of connection. But these guests are – for all that – benevolently indifferent. A trunk-fish ambles past on a search for algae without any curiosity or questions: everything seems allowed, no one would bat an eyelid.

Chiefly, they don't care: they don't know who the president is or who won the war. They particularly don't care about the gossip about us, our disappointed career ambitions and the frustrations in our relationship. The silvery porcupinefish has no thought of your brother; the yellowhead wrasse has no conception of envy. And we can appreciate them, for this total disregard for the demented human agenda.

We were as small children – amazed by everything; a light switch could detain us for hours. With maturity has come habituation and cynicism, yet still, the process does not have to go in only one direction. We are capable of returning to a less weary and blinkered place: we have a capacity for re-enchantment. And when it is engaged, we may notice, to our infinite and curative amazement, that in a universe composed chiefly of gas and rock circulating in the endless nothingness of space, a six-banded trevally has just swum below us in the warm ocean off Cachorro Beach on an eager search for a meal of cephalopods.

Conclusion

The hamlet of Gletsch, with the Rhône
glacier behind it, in 1900 and 2008.

'What need is there to weep over parts
of life?' knew the philosopher Seneca.
'The whole of it calls for tears.'

The Rhône Glacier

One of the more tragic sights we could cast our eyes on lies just outside the hamlet of Gletsch, in the upper Valais in the centre of Switzerland. The majestic Rhône glacier, which used to come right down into the settlement and could be seen from the elegant terrace of the Hôtel Glacier du Rhône, has now retreated several kilometres up the mountainside – melted remorselessly by the combined output of our boilers, hairdryers, farting cows, barbecues and steel mills. We might want to lie down in the rich alpine grass and weep without end.

The marks of our depredation are everywhere. The whole planet bears our scars. We have chopped at its forests, belched sulphuric acid into its rivers, murdered its blue whales and Siberian tigers, defaced its oceansides and darkened its skies. We struggle valiantly to apologise. We separate out our glass and our cardboard and try hard to remember to reuse our grocery bags. And yet this has some of the touching futility of attempting to stop a tank with a matchstick.

The ruination of the planet is not an incidental error into which we have somehow lapsed through inattention and technological over-enthusiasm: it is a direct and necessary consequence of who we are as people. The problem is psychological, not technical. If we are to put an end to our spoliation, we cannot simply pass a few regulations and add one or two taxes; we have to alter human nature. The issue we know as an environmental catastrophe is, once we swim a little upstream, in essence a moral crisis, an indictment of the core of our being. To heal the earth, we would need to change what we are like: we would have to overcome our rage, our greed, our paranoiac aggression, our stymied sympathy and our self-absorption. We would need to do what no religion, philosophy, psychotherapy or spiritual movement has ever managed to pull off since our emergence from the Rift Valley: turn us into substantially better people. The effort required to rewire our minds would dwarf that involved in trying to colonise a foreign galaxy.

Against such a backdrop, we should, in stronger moments, face up to a reality that – for touching and sentimental reasons – we keep skirting: we are unlikely to make it. The human experiment will one day run its course; our race will die out. Our chatter will eventually end. Our presses will fall silent. Our history will be erased under layers of sand and silt.

There will, of course, be much to regret. But after we have shed every last tear, we might look up from our grief with a certain stoic equanimity. That we won't make it will be a sign, definitive and unarguable, that we did not – in a key sense – merit doing so. Our characters were not up to the task. Our natures could not honour the stewardship we had been handed. There remained too much folly and anger in our skittish minds. We may feel sad; we do not have to feel betrayed or incensed.

We should, along the way, take comfort from the knowledge that we will be superseded by gentler or at least more modest life forms: by billions of arachnids and myriapods, crustaceans and bacteria. The odd snow leopard might wander among the ruins. Several million years from now, a wiser, cleverer, calmer, more peaceful higher primate might emerge, and feel pity and sorrow for all that we were.

We don't have to contemplate our residence on the planet on tenterhooks. After we have done everything we can, signed every petition, given up every harmful luxury, voted for every far-sighted politician, we can rest in the knowledge that we will either make it (and thereby prove our nobility) or we won't, thereby demonstrating beyond doubt or sadness that we didn't really deserve to.

Flooded fields and farmland beside
the River Cuckmere, following heavy
rain and high tides, Alfriston,
East Sussex, UK.

A huge number of reversals
should be expected in every good
and normal life.

Alfriston, Sussex

It looks – at first sight – like a terrifying disaster. The River Cuckmere, normally so placid and so picturesque, has ignored the limitations set down by nature, burst its banks and spread its flood waters and its mud across miles of ordinary countryside, inundating fields and footpaths where animals and humans only recently passed.

However, closer inspection and local knowledge reveal that this is nothing of the sort. The River Cuckmere lies in a long-established and well-marked floodplain. Rains and mud are expected here, not necessarily every year, but often enough. Acres of farmland have deliberately been left so that, should the river burst its banks after torrential rains and high tides, they can turn into gigantic lakes for a time without suffering any damage. The humans in the area have long memories, and they know what this apparently placid river can do. It might be quiescent for a while, but sure enough, it will flood once more – and woe to anyone who had thought of building themselves a house with a veranda, let alone setting up a power line, in such terrain.

There is, in this curious accommodation of the powers of nature, a psychological lesson on offer. A flood does not need to be the end, so long as we have prepared for it – have carefully dug drainage ditches, evacuated livestock and moved everything delicate onto higher ground. A good life is similarly one in which we can expect much to go wrong, and should not be banking on anything remaining trouble-free for long. The point isn't to try to avoid flood waters or to try to create impermeable dams to stop them. It's to cede to problems with grace when we need to and then mitigate their effects. We might have to surrender a lot of territory: the land around the River Cuckmere indicates as much. We might have to write off an entire portion of our lives. We might have to go to hospital or waste many days in bed, but we can do so in the knowledge that we were never assured an easier, unproblematic path.

Mental unwellness, terror, loneliness, loss and anguish belong to the business of living. We cannot hope to avoid them; we can only grow wise about how to drain and manage them. Not all the days in our diaries will be ours to enjoy; substantial numbers of them will be lost to despair and confusion. There should be nothing unusual or too painful in the thought. We can take courage from the example of those who work on the banks of the River Cuckmere; we should live with floodplains in our minds.

Astrid Reischwitz, *White Clouds*, from
'The Bedroom Project', 2013.

One of the finest of all possible
global destinations.

Bed

There are many places on the planet that offer us a therapeutic effect, but perhaps none that are, in the end, as much use to our psyches as this one. Our bed deserves to be recognised as the supreme location of reassurance, mental re-organisation and consolation. Were we unable to travel any distance beyond its limits, we would still have a world of reassurance at our fingertips.

A bed does not – of course – carry any overt glamour. We don't earn respect or interest for revealing that we have, once again, spent the weekend, or even the whole holidays, sleeping and reflecting under the duvet. A bed lacks the grandeur of the desert or the edifying ancient-ness of a past civilisation. And yet it may, at points, be exactly what we need to dampen our mania or make sense of our sadness.

A bed offers ideal conditions in which to think. It can be hard to do so properly at a desk. The mind may release its better thoughts only when we are horizontal and under little pressure to produce very much. It is then that our wilder, odder, more valuable ideas dare to make themselves felt – and we should be ready for them with an ample supply of notepads and pens. Thinking in bed, we can go back over a relationship, we can question our worries, we can push back against our self-doubt and impulses to self-sabotage.

At other times, thinking itself will be too much. As small children well know, there are moments when it may be most sensible simply to burst into tears. Away from frightening or shaming eyes, we can give way to sorrow in the bedclothes in a way we won't dare to in any other room. The pillows can absorb our tears, the duvet can muffle the crying. We can despair all that we need to: we can tell ourselves that nothing will ever be right, and that we have been a mistake from the very start. Exaggeration has its pleasures. And after a while of this form of limitless grief, we will be readier to return with perspective to our more hopeful thoughts. There might well be alternatives; there could be a way forward; a plan may start to emerge.

Often, we're brittle and desperate not because the problems are truly too large, but because we're simply too tired. The distinction is easy enough to observe in the case of children. A 3-year-old who throws their bowl of animal pasta on the floor and declares that they 'hate Mummy' isn't a monster, they're just exhausted. After a good night's sleep, they'll be a delight. We should extend the same kindly insight to our adult selves.

We can, in addition – at quieter moments – use our beds as tools of travel. They may be physically weighty, but they are nimble at carrying us back in time to journeys we have made and, without necessarily knowing it, minutely stored in our memories. When sleep refuses to come, we can journey back to summer evenings in the Mediterranean or to a friendship that we made in a foreign city. Far more remains than we might have imagined; as our bed teaches us, we don't always need to move our physical selves back to a place in order to feel as if we had returned to it.

The planet offers us so many places in which we can find healing. We should not neglect the one that we are (hopefully) already cosily ensconced in – or not too very far from.

List of Illustrations

p. 58   Robert Polidori, *Italian Painting 1300-1500 Gallery, J. Paul Getty Museum*, 1997. Chromogenic print. © Robert Polidori

p. 60   Hamish Fulton, *Road. Walking Away from Benicadell*, Spain, 2016. Image courtesy of Parafin, London. © Hamish Fulton

p. 64   Mojave Air and Space Port, California, USA, 2015. Photo AirTeamImages.com

p. 66   Massimo Vitali, *Constantine Arch Pine Tree*, 2008. © Massimo Vitali

p. 68   Swimming pool at deposed President Mobutu's private palace, Gbadolite, Democratic Republic of The Congo, January, 2015. Photo © Sean Smith / Guardian / eyevine

p. 70   Ornithomimidae skeleton, Central Museum of Mongolian Dinosaurs, Ulaanbaatar, Mongolia. Photo © Gary Todd / World History Photos

p. 72   Museum looted by ISIS in 2015, Palmyra, Syria. Photo © Torsten Pursche / Dreamstime.com

p. 74   Paige Lipsky, *Calvary Cemetery, Queens, with Manhattan Skyline*, 2017. © Paige Lipsky

p. 78   Albert Bierstadt, *Among the Sierra Nevada, California*, 1868. Oil on canvas, 183 × 305 cm. Smithsonian American Art Museum, Washington, D. C. Bequest of Helen Huntington Hull, granddaughter of William Brown Dinsmore, who acquired the painting in 1873 for "The Locusts," the family estate in Dutchess County, New York

p. 80   Aerial view of Meteor (Barringer) Crater, Arizona, USA. Photo © Chon Kit Leong / 123RF.com

p. 82   Huang Gongwang, *Dwelling in the Fuchun Mountains*, 1350 (detail). Scroll, ink on paper, 33 × 636.9 cm. National Palace Museum, Taipei, Taiwan

p. 84   The Gap lookout, Watsons Bay, Sydney, New South Wales, Australia. Photo Mehul Patel / Alamy Stock Photo

p. 88   Zebras migrating, Chobe National Park, Botswana. Photo © Frans Lanting / Lanting.com

p. 90   Combine harvesting of wheat, Saskatchewan, Canada. Photo Brian Martin / Alamy Stock Photo

p. 92   Maruyama Senmaida Rice Terraces at sunset, Kumano-shi, Mie Prefecture, Japan. Photo © Sean Pavone / 123RF.com

p. 94   Lemon grove orchard, Sicily, Italy. Photo © Tatiana Dyuvbanova / 123RF.com

p. 98   Salginatobel Bridge near Schiers, Switzerland. Photo Martin Bond / Alamy Stock Photo

p. 100   Edward Burtynsky, *Highway #1, Los Angeles, California, USA*, 2003. Photo © Edward Burtynsky, courtesy Flowers Gallery, London / Nicholas Metivier Gallery, Toronto

p. 102   Julian Hinds pumping plant, Colorado River Aqueduct, Hayfield Lake, California, USA, 2015. Photo Lucy Nicholson / Reuters / Alamy Stock Photo

p. 104   High Park Sewage Pumping Station, 195 Spring Road, Toronto, Canada. Photo taken in March, 2022. Photo © Paul Sergeant

p. 106   Killala Bay Cable Landing Station, Killala, County Mayo, Ireland. Photo courtesy AquaComms

p. 110   Jessie Scott, *Weatherboard Bungalow with Brick Cladding*, 2013. © Jessie Scott

p. 112   Mirko Rotondi, *Timeless Hotel, #18, Kuala Lumpur, Malaysia*, 2012. © Mirko Rotondi

p. 114   A cruise ship sails in the lagoon near St. Mark's Square, Venice, Italy, 2012. Photo Manuel Silvestri / Reuters / Alamy Stock Photo

p. 116   Garry Winogrand, *Paris, France*, c. 1969. © The Estate of Garry Winogrand, courtesy Fraenkel Gallery, San Francisco

p. 118   Edward Chao, *Illinois Center (Night), Mies and FFF, Chicago, IL*, 2018. © Edward Chao

p. 120   Oslo harbour with Oslo City Hall, Oslo, Norway, October, 1951. Photo Scanpix / NTB scanpix / akg-images

p. 122   Jean-Jacques Lorin, *Restaurant, Omoide Yokocho, Shinjuku, Tokyo*, 2016. Copyright © Jean-Jacques Lorin

p. 124   Bridge over the river, London, UK, January 2020. Photo Liang Zhao / EyeEm / Alamy Stock Photo

p. 126   Laurent Hou, *Sindorim Station, Seoul*, 2015. © Laurent Hou

p. 128   Garry Winogrand, *New York*, c. 1963. © The Estate of Garry Winogrand, courtesy Fraenkel Gallery, San Francisco

p. 132   San Juan River, Utah, USA. Photo Finetooth, 2010. Wikimedia Commons

p. 134   Arco di Riccardo, Trieste, Italy, 1st century CE. Photo bozac / Alamy Stock Photo

p. 136   Alcobaça Monastery, north of Lisbon, Portugal, founded in the 12th century CE by King Alfonso I. Photo © tupungato / 123RF.com

p. 138   *Océlotl Cuauhxicalli*, a jaguar-shaped stone vessel to hold the hearts of sacrificial victims, Aztec, late post-classic period, c. 1250–1500 CE. Andesite, 93.5 × 105 × 227 cm. National Museum of Anthropology, Mexico City, Mexico. Photo J. Enrique Molina / Album / akg-images

p. 140   Walker Evans, *City Lunch Counter, New York*, 1929. Museum of Modern Art (MoMA), New York. Gelatin silver print, 10.7 × 16.1cm. Gift of the artist (27.1994) © 2022. Digital Image, The Museum of Modern Art, New York / Scala, Florence. © Walker Evans Archive, The Metropolitan Museum of Art, New York

p. 144   Vincent Van Gogh, *Tree trunks in the grass, late April 1890*, 1890. Oil on canvas, 72.5 × 91.5 cm. Collection Kröller-Müller Museum, Otterlo, the Netherlands

p. 146   Patio de la Acequia, Palacio de Generalife, Alhambra Palace, Granada, Spain. Photo © Øyvind Holmstad (https://permaliv.myportfolio.com)

p. 150   Harald Sohlberg, *Våraften, Akershus (Spring Evening, Akershus)*, 1913. Oil on canvas, 82 × 114.5 cm. Oslo kommunes kunstsamlinger (City of Oslo Art Collection). Photo © Werner Zellien

p. 152   Night view of the VLT (Very Large Telescope) on the top of the Cerro Paranal in the heart of the Atacama Desert, Chile, July 17th, 2015, 03:04 am. Photo Alberto Ghizzi Panizza / ESO

p. 154   Adam Gold, *The View from the Window, London*, 2016. © Adam Gold

p. 156   Richard Misrach, *Untitled #213-04*, 2004. © Richard Misrach, courtesy Fraenkel Gallery, San Francisco

p. 160 (left)   The Rhône Glacier, Glacier Hotel and Furka Road, Valais, Swiss Alps. Photochrome published by the Detroit Publishing Co., c. 1900. Prints & Photographs Division, Library of Congress, Washington, D. C. (LC-DIG-ppmsc-07877)

p. 160 (right)   The hamlet of Gletsch, with the Rhône glacier behind it, 2008. Photo © Jürg Alean, Eglisau, Switzerland

p. 162   Cuckmere river in the South Downs National Park, England, UK, on a misty morning. Photo © Peter Cripps / 123RF.com

p. 164   Astrid Reischwitz, *White Clouds*, from 'The Bedroom Project', 2013. © Astrid Reischwitz 2013

Also available from The School of Life:

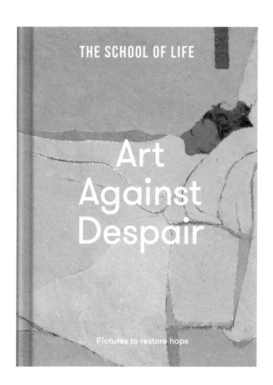

Art Against Despair

Pictures to restore hope

An inspiring selection of images offering us hope and comfort, reminding us that we are not alone in our sorrow.

One of the most unexpectedly useful things we can do when we're feeling glum or out of sorts is to look at pictures. The best works of art can lift our spirits, remind us of what we love and return perspective to our situation. A few moments in front of the right picture can rescue us.

This is a collection of the world's most consoling and uplifting images, accompanied by small essays that talk about the works in a way that offers us comfort and inspiration. The images in the book range wildly across time and space: from ancient to modern art, east to west, north to south, taking in photography, painting, abstract and figurative art. All the images have been carefully chosen to help us with a particular problem we might face: a broken heart, a difficulty at work, the meanness of others, the challenges of family and friends ... We're invited to look at art with unusual depth and then find our way towards new hope and courage.

This is a portable museum dedicated to beauty and consolation, a unique book about art which is also about psychology and healing: a true piece of art therapy.

ISBN: 978-1-912891-90-0

£22 | $32.99